Writer's Workbook

Level 4

A Division of The McGraw-Hill Companies

Columbus, Ohio

www.sra4kids.com

SRA/McGraw-Hill

A Division of The **McGraw·Hill** *Companies*

Copyright ©2002 by SRA/McGraw-Hill

Send all inquiries to:
SRA/McGraw-Hill
8787 Orion Place
Columbus, OH 43240-4027

Printed in the United States of America

ISBN 0-07-569548-0

5 6 7 8 9 QPD 06 05 04 03

Table of Contents

Autobiography

Objective: Students prewrite for an autobiography.

Use the writing process to write an autobiography.

Prewriting

Who is the audience for your autobiography?

☐ Your teacher

☐ Classmates

☐ Your family

☐ Other _____

What is your purpose for writing?

☐ To inform others about one special event in your life

☐ To tell about your entire life

☐ To tell about something funny that happened in your life

☐ Other _____

Write your ideas for the event or events you might include in your autobiography.

_____

_____

_____

_____

_____

_____

Name _____ Date _____

Autobiography

Use the graphic organizer to write the events in the order in which they happened.

Objective: Students prewrite and draft an autobiography.

THE WRITING PROCESS

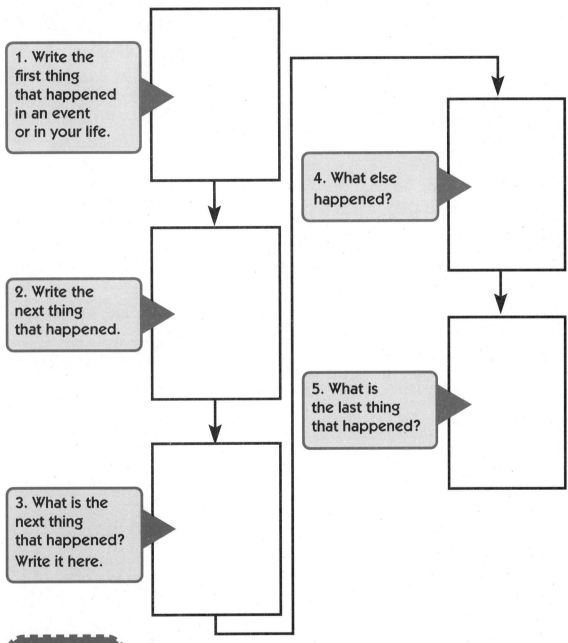

1. Write the first thing that happened in an event or in your life.

2. Write the next thing that happened.

3. What is the next thing that happened? Write it here.

4. What else happened?

5. What is the last thing that happened?

Drafting

Write the first draft of your autobiography on loose-leaf paper. Follow your graphic organizer to make sure you stay on topic. Keep your draft in your Writing Folder.

Name _____ Date _____

▸ **Autobiography**

Objective: Students revise an autobiography.

Revising

Read your autobiography draft. Use this checklist to improve your writing. Mark any changes to your draft using proofreading marks.

Ideas

☐ Is the main idea in each paragraph supported by details?

Organization

☐ Do you present events in your autobiography in the order in which they actually occurred?

Word Choice

☐ Do you use words such as *first*, *next*, and *last* that show the order of events in your autobiography?

Sentence Fluency

☐ Do the verbs agree with the subjects in your sentences?

☐ Do you use the pronoun *I* correctly in your sentences?

Voice

☐ Does your autobiography sound like you?

☐ Other _____

Revise your paper. You may need to rewrite your autobiography, making all the changes you marked in your paper.

Proofreading Marks	
¶	Indent.
∧	Add something.
ℯ	Take something out.
∼	Transpose.
≡	Make a capital letter.
/	Make a small letter.
◯	Check spelling.
⊂	Close up space.
#	Add space.
⊙	Add a period.

Objective: Students edit, proofread, and publish an autobiography.

THE WRITING PROCESS

▶ **Autobiography**

Editing/Proofreading

It is important to proofread your revised draft. Your final copy should be error-free. Use this checklist to make sure you remember to check everything.

Conventions

☐ Make sure that all words are spelled correctly.

☐ Check all punctuation to make sure it is correct.

☐ Make sure that each sentence and all proper nouns begin with a capital letter.

☐ Read aloud to catch grammar errors such as sentence fragments and run-on sentences.

☐ Other _____

Publishing

Use this checklist to get your autobiography ready for publication.

Presentation

☐ If working on a computer, print a final copy on white paper. If handwriting, write a final copy on white paper.

☐ Read your work one more time. Neatly correct any errors you made in the final copy.

☐ You can make your autobiography into a book and include illustrations or photographs. See *Language Arts Handbook* page 48 for directions on binding your own book.

Name _____ Date _____

Explaining a Process

Use the writing process to explain a process.

Prewriting

Who is the audience for your process?

☐ Your teacher

☐ An adult in your family

☐ Your sister, brother, or cousin

☐ Someone interested in starting a business

☐ People in your neighborhood

☐ Your classmates

☐ Other _____

What is your purpose for writing?

☐ To explain the process of starting a dog-walking business

☐ To explain the process of starting a yard-cleaning business

☐ To explain the process of starting a grocery-delivery business

☐ Other _____

Write the type of business you will write about here.

_____

_____

_____

_____

_____

Name _____ Date _____

Explaining a Process

Objective: Prewrite and draft an explanation of a process.

Use the graphic organizer to write the steps in the process you are explaining. Write the steps in the correct sequence.

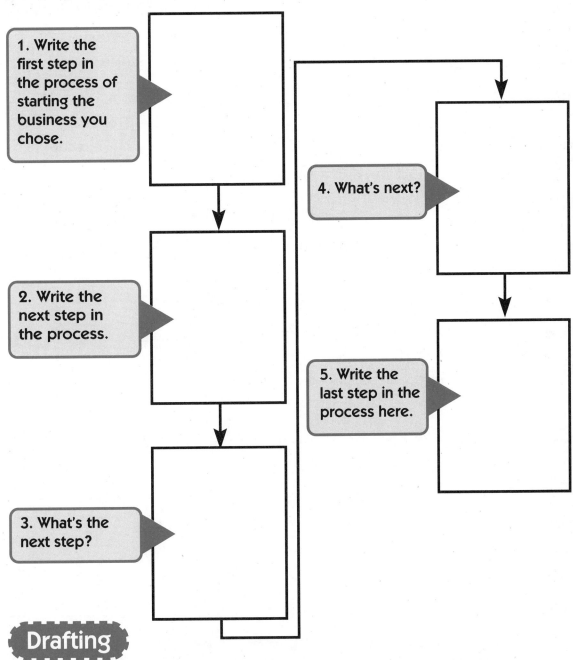

1. Write the first step in the process of starting the business you chose.

2. Write the next step in the process.

3. What's the next step?

4. What's next?

5. Write the last step in the process here.

Drafting

Write the first draft of your explanation on loose-leaf paper. Follow your graphic organizer to make sure you stay on topic. Keep your draft in your Writing Folder.

UNIT 2   Dollars and Sense • **Lesson I** *Starting a Business*

▶ **Explaining a Process**

Objective: Revise an explanation of a process.

Revising

Read your explanation carefully. Use this checklist to make it clearer. Use proofreading marks to show any needed changes.

Ideas

☐ Is each step clearly written?

☐ Have you left out any important steps or information?

Organization

☐ Have you written a short introduction to tell readers what you are explaining?

☐ Are the steps described in sequential order?

☐ Have you added a short conclusion to your explanation?

Word Choice

☐ Did you include words that show the order of the steps in the process?

☐ Did you name any parts or tools correctly?

Sentence Fluency

☐ Does each sentence lead to the next one, with no sudden jumps from one topic to a new one?

Voice

☐ Do you explain why this process is important to readers?

☐ Does your explanation show that you are interested in this process?

☐ Other _____

	Proofreading Marks
¶	Indent.
∧	Add something.
℮	Take something out.
∼	Transpose.
≡	Make a capital letter.
/	Make a small letter.
sp	Check spelling.
⊂	Close up space.
⋏#	Add space.
⊙	Add a period.

Make the changes you marked in your paper. Rewrite your explanation on loose-leaf paper or on a computer. Keep a copy in your Writing Folder.

▶ **Explaining a Process**

EXPOSITORY WRITING

Editing/Proofreading

Be sure to proofread your explanation. Make sure your readers can follow it. If possible, have someone else read your explanation and tell you whether it is clear.

Conventions

☐ Do you use commas correctly in compound and complex sentences?

☐ Do all your sentences have the correct end punctuation?

☐ Does each sentence start with a capital letter, even if you organized your explanation in numbered steps?

☐ Did you check your spelling, even if you used a computer spell checker?

☐ Other _____

Publishing

Use this checklist to get your explanation ready for readers.

Presentation

☐ Handwrite or type a clean copy of your explanation.

☐ Check the format. Make sure your readers can find and follow each step in the process you explain.

☐ Include a diagram or other illustration to help readers understand the process.

☐ Share your explanation with others. Publish a newsletter with your classmates about businesses that kids could create and manage.

☐ If you write about how to start a dog-walking business, do it! You might need help from your parents or your teacher before you start your business.

☐ Other _____

Summary Paragraph

Use the writing process to write a summary paragraph.

Prewriting

Who is the audience for your summary?

☐ Your teacher

☐ Yourself

☐ A classmate

☐ Readers interested in the book or story you are summarizing

☐ Other _____

What is your purpose for writing?

☐ To explain the main idea in a book about starting a business

☐ To explain the main idea in a story or magazine article about starting a business

☐ To explain the main idea in "Henry Wells and . . . William G. Fargo"

☐ Other _____

Write the title and the author of the book, story, or article that you are summarizing. Read it a few times, if you can, before you begin to write.

Title _____

_____

Author _____

► **Summary Paragraph**

EXPOSITORY WRITING

Objective: Prewrite and draft a summary paragraph.

Use the graphic organizer to write the main idea and details in the book, story, or article.

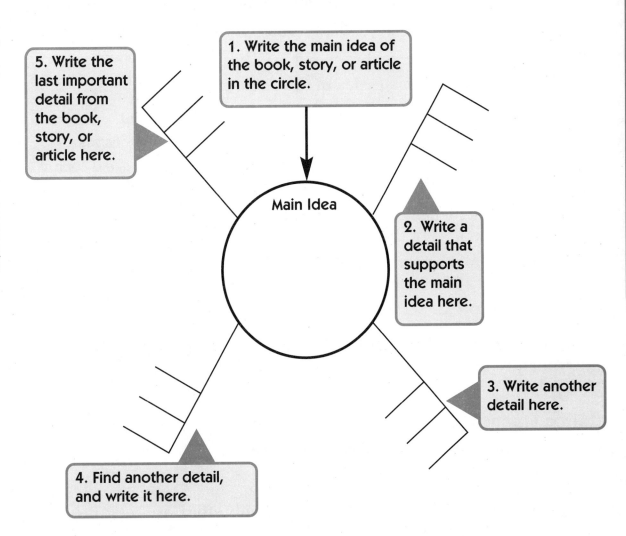

5. Write the last important detail from the book, story, or article here.

1. Write the main idea of the book, story, or article in the circle.

Main Idea

2. Write a detail that supports the main idea here.

3. Write another detail here.

4. Find another detail, and write it here.

Drafting

Write the first draft of your summary paragraph on loose-leaf paper. Use your graphic organizer to write the main idea and the most important details in your summary paragraph. Remember to write in complete sentences and indent the paragraph. Keep your draft in your Writing Folder.

UNIT 2   Dollars and Sense • **Lesson 2** *Henry Wells and . . . William G. Fargo*

Summary Paragraph

Revising

Read your summary paragraph carefully. Use this checklist to improve your writing. Mark any errors with proofreading marks.

Ideas

☐ Do you write about the main idea of the book, story, or article you read?

☐ Do you include only the most important details in your summary?

Organization

☐ Does the topic sentence of your summary explain the main idea of the selection?

☐ Do the other sentences in the paragraph support the main idea?

Word Choice

☐ Have you chosen the best words to explain the main idea and details in the book, story, or article?

Sentence Fluency

☐ Do you combine short sentences when possible?

Voice

☐ Can the reader tell that you have read the book, story, or article you summarized?

☐ Other _____

If you have made many changes, rewrite your summary paragraph by hand or on a computer.

Proofreading Marks	
¶	Indent.
∧	Add something.
ℯ	Take something out.
∼	Transpose.
≡	Make a capital letter.
/	Make a small letter.
⌢sp	Check spelling.
◡	Close up space.
#⌃	Add space.
⊙	Add a period.

Objective: Revise a summary paragraph.

▶ **Summary Paragraph**

Objective: Edit, proofread, and publish a summary paragraph.

EXPOSITORY WRITING

Editing/Proofreading

Be sure to proofread your summary. Use this checklist to make sure your paper is free of errors.

Conventions

☐ Do you use capital letters correctly in titles, the first word of each sentence, and proper nouns?

☐ Are commas and other punctuation used correctly?

☐ Did you check your spelling, even if you used a computer spell checker?

☐ Are pronouns used correctly and in agreement with their antecedents in number and gender?

☐ Do you use singular verbs with singular subjects and plural verbs with plural subjects?

☐ Other _____

Publishing

Use this checklist to get your summary ready for other readers.

Presentation

☐ Handwrite or type a clean copy of your summary.

☐ Share your summary with others. You and your classmates might combine summaries of similar selections into folders. Label each folder to tell readers what kind of summaries it contains. Put the folders in your school library or classroom for others to read and use for a book or research report.

☐ Other _____

Writing a News Story

Use the writing process to write a news story.

Prewriting

Who is the audience for your story?

☐ Students in your class

☐ People in your community

☐ People who own and run businesses in your neighborhood

☐ Other _____

What is your purpose for writing?

☐ To tell readers about a businessperson in your neighborhood

☐ To explain how someone started a new business

☐ To explain how a businessperson in your community became successful

☐ To tell about a person who has owned and operated a business for many years

☐ Other _____

Interview the businessperson you are writing about in your news story. Fill in information below.

Person to interview _____

Type of business _____

Questions to ask _____

_____

_____

▶ **Writing a News Story**

EXPOSITORY WRITING

Objective: Prewrite and draft a news story.

Plan the lead, the body, and the close of your news story. Decide how to organize the main points of the story.

1. Write the lead paragraph here. The first sentence should answer the questions *What*? *When*? *Where*? *Who*? The next one or two sentences should answer the question *Why*?

2. This paragraph begins the body. Write the most important details here.

3. Write the next most important details here.

4. Write the least important detail here.

5. Write the closing here. End with a sentence or two that summarizes the story or includes your observations.

Drafting

Write the first draft of your news story on loose-leaf paper. Make sure you include all parts of a news story in your draft. Add the headline and the byline.

UNIT 2   Dollars and Sense • **Lesson 3** *Elias Sifuentes, Restaurateur*

Objective: Revise a news story.

Revising

Writing a News Story

Read your news story carefully, answering the questions on this checklist. Use proofreading marks to show any needed changes.

Ideas

☐ Did you tell who, what, when, where, and why in your news story?

☐ Have you clearly explained why you wrote about this person?

Organization

☐ Is the lead to your news story interesting?

☐ Did you organize the background information in the body in a logical way?

☐ Have you ended with a sentence that summarizes your story or includes your observations?

Word Choice

☐ Have you used specific, interesting words instead of general ones?

☐ Did you delete unnecessary words?

Sentence Fluency

☐ Did you use active voice in your sentences?

Voice

☐ Will the subject of your news story interest your audience?

☐ Does your story show that you admire this person?

☐ Other _____

Mark all the errors in your news story using proofreading marks. If you have made many changes, rewrite your news story by hand or on a computer.

Proofreading Marks

¶	Indent.
∧	Add something.
ℓ	Take something out.
∽	Transpose.
≡	Make a capital letter.
/	Make a small letter.
	Check spelling.
⊂	Close up space.
#	Add space.
⊙	Add a period.

▶ **Writing a News Story**

Objective: Edit, proofread, and publish a news story.

Editing/Proofreading

Be sure to proofread your news story. Make sure you used the conventions of writing correctly in your news story.

Conventions

☐ Are the names of the people in your story spelled correctly?

☐ Have you checked the spelling in the rest of your story?

☐ Are the quotations punctuated correctly?

☐ Does each sentence end with the correct punctuation mark?

☐ Do you include periods after some abbreviations?

☐ Other _____

Publishing

Use this checklist to get your news story ready for readers.

Presentation

☐ Make sure your writing is neat, with no crossed-out words or other mistakes.

☐ Include a photograph or illustration of your subject if possible.

☐ Share your news story with others. Submit your news story to the school or community newspaper for publication. You might create your own newsletter with your classmates.

☐ Other _____

EXPOSITORY WRITING

Name _____ Date _____

UNIT 2 Dollars and Sense • **Lesson 4** *Food From the 'Hood*

Writing About Nonfiction

Use the writing process to respond to nonfiction.

Prewriting

Who is the audience for your response?

☐ Your teacher

☐ Your classmates

☐ Someone who has a vegetable garden

☐ Someone who sells vegetables

☐ Other _____

What is your purpose for writing?

☐ To explain an article or book about organic farming

☐ To explain an article or book about how to grow a
   vegetable garden

☐ Other _____

**Write your ideas about the article or book you've read
about farming or gardening. Write the main idea,
details from the article or book, and what you already
know about the subject in the space below.**

_____

_____

_____

_____

_____

_____

Writing About Nonfiction • **Writer's Workbook**

Objective: Prewrite an expository paper about a nonfiction text.

Name _____ Date _____

Objective: Prewrite and draft an expository paper about a nonfiction text.

UNIT 2 Dollars and Sense • **Lesson 4** *Food From the 'Hood*

▶ Writing About Nonfiction

EXPOSITORY WRITING

Use the Venn diagram to organize some of the details about farming or gardening you might compare and contrast in your response.

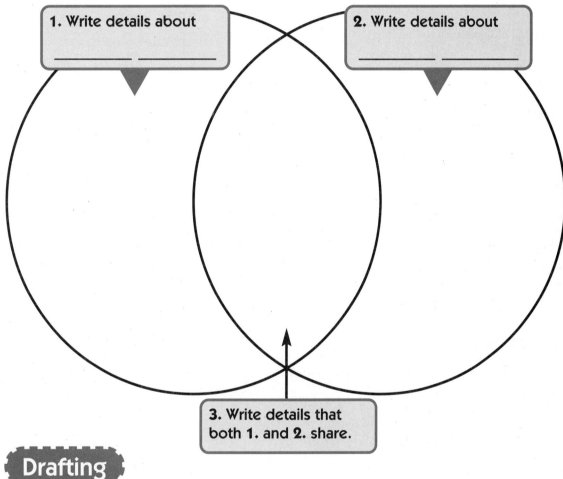

1. Write details about
_____ _____

2. Write details about
_____ _____

3. Write details that both **1.** and **2.** share.

Drafting

Write the first draft of your response on loose-leaf paper. Write in complete sentences and group your sentences into paragraphs. Keep your draft in your Writing Folder.

Writer's Workbook • *Writing About Nonfiction*   UNIT 2 • Lesson 4   **19**

Objective: Revise an expository paper about a nonfiction text.

▶ **Writing About Nonfiction**

Revising

Read your response carefully. Use this checklist to make your ideas clearer.

Ideas

☐ Have you clearly explained how the two ideas are the same and different?

☐ Does your response show that you have carefully read and thought about this reading selection?

Organization

☐ Have you begun with a topic sentence that tells the reader what is ahead?

☐ Have you added a short conclusion to your response?

Word Choice

☐ Did you include words that are specific and precise so that readers will understand your points?

☐ Did you use words that are familiar to your readers?

Sentence Fluency

☐ Have you used a combination of short, medium, and long sentences?

☐ Have you used words and phrases such as *however* and *for example* to show how your ideas are related to each other?

Voice

☐ Does your response express your surprise about what you learned from this selection?

☐ Other _____

If you have made many changes, rewrite your paper by hand or on a computer.

Proofreading Marks	
¶	Indent.
∧	Add something.
℮	Take something out.
∼	Transpose.
≡	Make a capital letter.
/	Make a small letter.
sp	Check spelling.
⊃⊂	Close up space.
∧#	Add space.
⊙	Add a period.

UNIT 2 Dollars and Sense • **Lesson 4** *Food From the 'Hood*

▶ **Writing About Nonfiction**

Objective: Edit, proofread, and publish an expository paper about a nonfiction text.

Editing/Proofreading

Be sure to proofread your response. Readers often think that careless mistakes are a sign of careless thinking.

Conventions

☐ Did you use commas correctly in a series and in dates?

☐ Did you use other punctuation in your sentences correctly?

☐ Did you begin all proper nouns with capital letters?

☐ Did you check your spelling, even if you used a computer spell checker?

☐ Other _____

Publishing

Use this checklist to get your response ready for readers.

Presentation

☐ Handwrite or type your response. Make sure you indent your paragraphs.

☐ Share your response with others. You can publish your response in a magazine. Mail a copy to a magazine publisher or make your own with your classmates.

☐ Other _____

Writing a Research Report

Objective: Prewrite a research report.

Use the writing process to write a research report.

Prewriting

Who is the audience for your report?

☐ Your teacher

☐ A person who owns a business

☐ Other _____ _____

What is your purpose for writing?

☐ To inform readers about the history of supermarkets

☐ To tell about the first businesses that opened in your town or city

☐ Other _____

Fill in information about your research.

Topic _____

What I need to know about my topic _____

_____

_____

_____

Next, gather information about your topic. Take notes on the information.

Name _____ Date _____

► **Writing a Research Report**

Gather the notes about your topic. Use this graphic organizer to organize the information and ideas from your research.

Objective: Prewrite and draft a research report.

EXPOSITORY WRITING

Topic [ ]
◄ **1.** Write the topic of your research report here.

Subtopic [ ]
_____
_____
◄ **2.** Write the subtopics that support the main topic in the three boxes.

Subtopic [ ]
_____
_____
◄ **3.** Write details for the subtopics under each box.

Subtopic [ ]
_____
_____

Conclusion [ ]
◄ **4.** Write the conclusion to your research report here.

Drafting

Turn your ideas into sentences. Write the first draft on loose-leaf paper and keep in your **Writing Folder**.

Objective: Revise a research report.

▶ **Writing a Research Report**

Revising

Read your report carefully. Use this checklist to make it clearer and better organized. Use proofreading marks to show any needed changes.

Ideas

☐ Do you use information from up-to-date sources?

☐ Do the subtopics and details that you included support your main idea or topic?

Organization

☐ Did your introduction explain your topic and what you will cover?

☐ Did you organize the subtopics in a logical order?

☐ Have you ended with a conclusion based on your research?

Word Choice

☐ Do you define any terms that might be unfamiliar to your readers?

Sentence Fluency

☐ Does each sentence lead to the next one, with no sudden jumps in topic?

Voice

☐ Will readers know that this research topic is important to you?

☐ Other _____

If you have made many changes, rewrite your report by hand or on a computer.

Proofreading Marks	
¶	Indent.
∧	Add something.
ℓ	Take something out.
∼	Transpose.
≡	Make a capital letter.
/	Make a small letter.
sp ◯	Check spelling.
⊂	Close up space.
#	Add space.
⊙	Add a period.

UNIT 2 Dollars and Sense • **Lesson 5** *Business Is Looking Up*

▶ **Writing a Research Report**

Editing/Proofreading

Be sure to proofread your report. Misspellings and other mistakes can lead readers to question your conclusions.

Conventions

☐ If you used a direct quote, did you use quotation marks correctly?

☐ Do you use quotation marks and underlining correctly in titles?

☐ Is your other punctuation correct?

☐ Does each sentence and proper noun start with a capital letter?

☐ Did you check your spelling, especially names and titles?

☐ Other _____

Publishing

Use this checklist to get your report ready for readers.

Presentation

☐ Handwrite or type a clean copy of your research report. Make sure your paragraphs are indented.

☐ Include a diagram, photograph, or other illustration to help readers understand your topic.

☐ Give an oral presentation of your research report to your class. Use illustrations, charts, diagrams, or tables in your presentation.

☐ You might consider publishing your research report in the school newspaper or a community newsletter.

☐ Other _____

EXPOSITORY WRITING

Writing a Book Review

Objective: Prewrite a book review.

Use the writing process to write a book review.

Prewriting

Who is the audience for your review?

☐ Your teacher

☐ Your family

☐ People who use your local public library

☐ The school librarian or media specialist

☐ Other students at school

☐ Other _____

What is your purpose for writing?

☐ To inform readers about a book

☐ To persuade readers to read the book

☐ Other _____

Fill in information about the book you are reviewing.

Title _____

Author _____

Date of Publication _____

Type of book _____

Name _____ Date _____

▶ **Writing a Book Review**

EXPOSITORY WRITING

Use this graphic organizer to organize your review.
After writing the subtopics in the small boxes, list any
details you want to include on the lines underneath.

Objective: Prewrite and draft a book review.

Topic [   ]

1. Write the topic of your literature response here.

Subtopic [   ]

_____

_____

2. Write the subtopics that support the main topic in the three boxes.

Subtopic [   ]

_____

_____

3. Write details under each box.

Subtopic [   ]

_____

_____

Conclusion [   ]

4. Write ___ conclusion to ___ literature response here.

Drafting

Write the first draft of your review on loose-leaf paper.
Follow your graphic organizer. Keep your draft in your
Writing Folder.

Revising

Read your review carefully. Use this checklist to make it clearer and more interesting. Use proofreading marks to show any needed changes.

Ideas

☐ Do you include the most important details about the plot, characters, and setting in your review of the book?

☐ Do you explain your opinion of the book clearly and offer supporting details?

Organization

☐ Do you begin by giving basic information about the book?

☐ Do you end with a brief conclusion?

Word Choice

☐ Do you use specific words and phrases to give readers a clear picture of the book?

☐ Do you avoid using words that readers might not understand unless they have read the book?

Sentence Fluency

☐ Did you read your review aloud and listen for any awkward phrases?

Voice

☐ Does your writing show your feelings about the book you reviewed?

☐ Other _____

If you have made many changes, rewrite your book review by hand or on a computer. Keep a copy of your review in your Writing Folder.

Proofreading Marks	
¶	Indent.
∧	Add something.
ℓ	Take something out.
~	Transpose.
≡	Make a capital letter.
/	Make a small letter.
﹩◯	Check spelling.
⌒	Close up space.
#	Add space.
⊙	Add a period.

Objective: Revise a book review.

▶ **Writing a Book Review**

Objective: Edit, proofread, and publish a book review.

Editing/Proofreading

Be sure to proofread your book review. If you miss any mistakes, they might draw readers' attention away from your review.

Conventions

☐ Do you spell and capitalize all the names, titles, and places correctly?

☐ Do you use colons, semicolons, and other punctuation marks correctly?

☐ Does each sentence start with a capital letter?

☐ Do the verbs in your sentences agree with their subjects?

☐ Other _____

Publishing

Use this checklist to get your review ready for readers.

Presentation

☐ Make all necessary corrections. Then, handwrite or type a clean copy of your book review.

☐ Share your review with others. Do an oral presentation of your book review. Your audience can be students in your class or other children at a public library. Bring a copy of the book to show your audience during your presentation.

☐ You might publish a copy of your review for your school library, classroom, or media resource room. You and your classmates can put copies of your book reviews in a folder for others to read.

☐ Other _____

EXPOSITORY WRITING

Writing About Fiction

Use the writing process to write about fiction.

Prewriting

Who is the audience for this response to fiction?

☐ Your teacher

☐ Your classmates

☐ A friend

☐ Someone who has read the same work of fiction that you are writing about in your response

☐ Other _____

What is your purpose for writing?

☐ To explain a theme, such as Dollars and Sense, in a work of fiction

☐ To analyze the main character of a story

☐ To analyze the plot of a story

☐ Other _____

Fill in the information below about your literature response.

Title of book or story _____

My ideas about the book _____

_____

_____

_____

▶ **Writing About Fiction**

Objective: Prewrite and draft an expository paper about a work of fiction.

EXPOSITORY WRITING

Use this graphic organizer to organize your response to the book or story you selected.

Topic

> **1.** Write the topic of your literature response here.

Subtopic

> **2.** Write the subtopics that support the main topic in the three boxes.

Subtopic

> **3.** Write details under each box.

Subtopic

Conclusion

> **4.** Write the conclusion to your literature response here.

Drafting

Write the first draft of your response on loose-leaf paper. Write your ideas in sentences and paragraphs. Keep a copy in your **Writing Folder.**

UNIT 2   Dollars and Sense • **Lesson 7** *The Milkmaid and Her Pail*

Objective: Revise an expository paper about a work of fiction.

> **Writing About Fiction**

Revising

Read your response carefully. This checklist can help you make it clearer and better organized. Use proofreading marks to show any needed changes.

Ideas

☐ Are your ideas about the theme, character, or plot in the book or story clear?

☐ Do you support your opinion with details from the selection and from your own experience?

Organization

☐ Does your introduction let the reader know what the topic of your paper is?

☐ Does your response end with a conclusion that sums up your thoughts and ideas?

Word Choice

☐ Do you use words that create a clear picture of your ideas about a character or the plot?

☐ Do you use some synonyms instead of repeating the same words?

Sentence Fluency

☐ Have you included short, medium, and long sentences?

Voice

☐ Does your writing show that you are interested in the book or story you write about in your response?

☐ Other _____

If you have made many changes, rewrite your response by hand or on a computer.

Proofreading Marks	
¶	Indent.
∧	Add something.
ℓ	Take something out.
∼	Transpose.
≡	Make a capital letter.
/	Make a small letter.
sp ◯	Check spelling.
◡	Close up space.
#	Add space.
⊙	Add a period.

Name ________________________________ Date ____________

Writing About Fiction

EXPOSITORY WRITING

Objective: Edit, proofread, and publish an expository paper about a work of fiction.

Editing/Proofreading

Be sure to proofread your response. Misspellings and other mistakes can distract readers from your message.

Conventions

- ☐ Did you include simple, compound, and complex sentences—and punctuate them correctly?
- ☐ Does each sentence, proper noun, and title start with a capital letter?
- ☐ Did you use end punctuation and commas correctly?
- ☐ Did you use quotation marks, colons, semicolons, and other marks correctly?
- ☐ Did you check your spelling, especially names and titles?
- ☐ Other ________________________________

Publishing

Use this checklist to get your response ready for readers.

Presentation

- ☐ Write or type a clean copy of your response. Make sure it is neat and your paragraphs are indented. Your left and right margins should be even, too.
- ☐ Give your paper a title that tells the reader what the topic is.
- ☐ Share your response with others. You and your classmates can bind your responses together as a literary journal. This journal could be placed in the school library or kept in the classroom for other students to read.
- ☐ Other ________________________________

Writing a Business Letter

Objective: Students prewrite a business letter.

Use the writing process to organize and write a business letter.

Prewriting

Who is the *audience* for your letter?

☐ Your teacher

☐ An administrator at a hospital

☐ A president of a health organization

☐ A doctor or a nurse at a health clinic

☐ Other _____

What is your *purpose* for writing?

☐ To ask for information about a local hospital

☐ To ask for information about a health organization, such as the American Medical Association

☐ Other _____

Fill in information about the organization you chose. Identify a specific person to receive your letter.

Person's name: _____

Name of the group or organization: _____

_____

Street address: _____

City: _____ State: _____ Zip Code: _____

UNIT 3 From Mystery to Medicine • **Lesson I** *Medicine: Past and Present*

▶ **Writing a Business Letter**

Objective: Students prewrite and draft a business letter.

PERSONAL WRITING

Organize your ideas for your letter. Make sure you include your request for information and why you need it in the body.

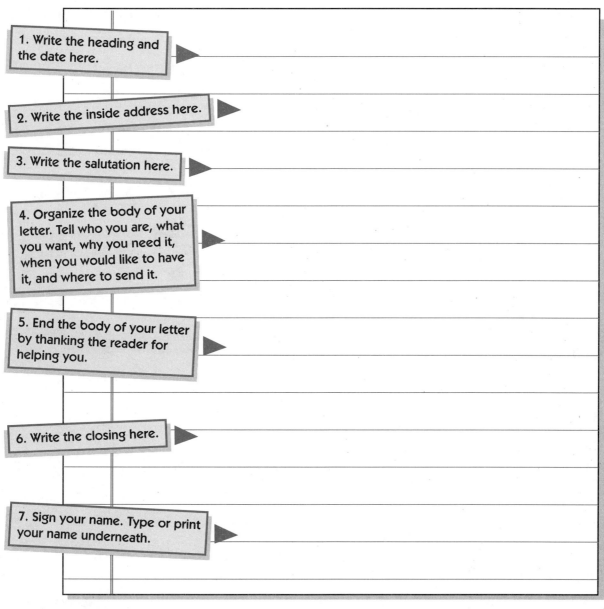

1. Write the heading and the date here.

2. Write the inside address here.

3. Write the salutation here.

4. Organize the body of your letter. Tell who you are, what you want, why you need it, when you would like to have it, and where to send it.

5. End the body of your letter by thanking the reader for helping you.

6. Write the closing here.

7. Sign your name. Type or print your name underneath.

Drafting

Write the first draft of your letter on loose-leaf paper or on a computer. Turn the ideas in the body of your letter into complete sentences.

Objective: Students revise a business letter.

▶ **Writing a Business Letter**

Revising

Read your letter carefully. You want to make a good impression on your reader. Use this checklist to make your letter clearer, and use proofreading marks to show any needed changes.

Ideas

☐ Is your request specific and clear?

☐ Did you explain why you need this information?

Organization

☐ Did you begin by telling who you are and what you want?

☐ Did the other sentences in your letter tell the reasons for your request?

☐ Did you end by thanking your reader?

Word Choice

☐ Should you replace any words with more specific ones?

Sentence Fluency

☐ Did you use short, medium, and long sentences?

☐ When you read your letter aloud, do any sentences sound awkward?

Voice

☐ Did you explain why receiving this information is important to you?

☐ When you thank the reader, does it sound as if you really mean it?

☐ Other _____

If you have made many changes, rewrite your business letter on loose-leaf paper or on a computer.

Proofreading Marks	
¶	Indent.
∧	Add something.
ℯ	Take something out.
∽	Transpose.
≡	Make a capital letter.
/	Make a small letter.
⌇	Check spelling.
⊂⊃	Close up space.
#	Add space.
⊙	Add a period.

▶ **Writing a Business Letter**

Editing/Proofreading

Be sure to proofread your letter. Your reader will notice any mistakes in it. Checking the items on this list can help you make a good impression.

Conventions

☐ Make sure you spelled names, titles, and addresses correctly.

☐ Check the punctuation in your heading, inside address, salutation, and closing.

☐ Make sure each sentence and proper noun starts with a capital letter.

☐ Check your spelling, even if you used a computer spell-checker. You can use spelling strategies and a dictionary to check your spelling.

☐ Other _____

Publishing

Use this checklist to get your letter ready to mail.

☐ Make sure your typing or writing is neat, with no crossed-out words.

☐ Sign your letter.

☐ Address and proofread the envelope. Make sure the address is correct and matches the heading on your letter.

☐ Add your return address to the envelope.

☐ Give your letter to your teacher to mail, or add a stamp and mail it yourself.

☐ Other _____

PERSONAL WRITING

Objective: Students edit, proofread, and publish a business letter.

Objective: Students practice writing in a personal journal.

UNIT 3 From Mystery to Medicine • **Lesson 2** *Sewed Up His Heart*

Writing in a Personal Journal

Practice writing entries in a personal journal.

Journal Entry 1

Who or What Is Your Subject?

Write a journal entry about a person you know in medicine. The person might be your family doctor or your school's nurse. You can write your journal entry on this page or in your Writer's Notebook.

My subject: _____

1. Write today's date here. ▶

2. Write the name of the doctor or nurse and how you know him or her. ▶

3. Describe how the person looks. Write your description here. ▶

4. Write how the person acts or behaves here. ▶

► Writing in a Personal Journal

Objective: Students practice writing in a personal journal.

PERSONAL WRITING

Journal Entry 2

What Does Your Subject Do?

Tell more about the doctor or nurse you wrote about in your first journal entry. Write another journal entry and include more details about what type of work he or she does and where. Describe the place of work in detail, using place and location words. You can write your journal entry on this page or in your Writer's Notebook.

1. Write today's date here. ▶

2. Write details about what the doctor or nurse does. Include answers to these questions in your entry.
• What kinds of tasks does this person do every day?
• Which tasks seem to be difficult? Why? ▶

3. Write a detailed description of the office where the doctor or nurse works. Are there others who work in the same office? Include them in your description. Use place and location words to show where objects and people usually are in the doctor's or nurse's office. ▶

Name _____ Date _____

Objective: Students practice writing in a personal journal.

Journal Entry 3

Why Is Your Subject Special or Important?

Why is the doctor or nurse you wrote about in your journal important to you? Write details in another journal entry explaining why the doctor or nurse you wrote about is important or special. You can write your journal entry on this page or in your Writer's Notebook.

1. Write today's date here. ►

2. Explain why the doctor or nurse is an important or special person. Give examples of what he or she has done for you and others. ►

▶ **Writing in a Personal Journal**

PERSONAL WRITING

Objective: Students practice writing in a personal journal.

Journal Entry 4

What Are Your Thoughts about Your Subject?

Think about the doctor or nurse you wrote about in your journal entry this week. What thoughts come to your mind? What special experiences do you remember? Write your thoughts about the doctor or nurse here or in your Writer's Notebook. Finish the statements below to help you write your thoughts.

1. Write today's date here. ▶

2. Choose and finish one or more of the statements below. Include the "answers" in your journal entry.
• I really admire this person's ability to ___.
• I will never forget the time this person ___.
• This person has helped me learn ___.
• I would like to tell this person ___.
• I am glad I know this person because ___.

▶

Objective: Students practice writing in a literature response journal.

Writing in a Literature Response Journal

Practice writing entries in a literature response journal.

Journal Entry 1

Responding to the Setting

Write your ideas about the setting of a book or story you have read. Answer the questions to help you write your journal entry. You can write your entry on this page or in your Writer's Notebook.

Write the title and the author of the book or story.

_____

_____

1. Write today's date here.

2. Answer one or more of the following questions to help you write your response to the setting.
• How would you describe the setting?
• Does the setting change during the story? How?
• How does the setting affect the story? Could the story have taken place in another setting? Why or why not?
• Would you like to live in or visit the setting of this story or book? Why or why not?

▶ **Writing in a Literature Response Journal**

PERSONAL WRITING

Objective: Students practice writing in a literature response journal.

Journal Entry 2

Responding to a Character

Write your thoughts in a journal entry about one of the main characters in the story you've chosen. Answer the questions below to help you write your response. You can write your entry on this page or in your Writer's Notebook.

Write the name of one of the main characters in the story or

book you've chosen. _____

1. Write today's date here. ▶

2. Describe the character you have chosen. Answer the following questions about him or her in your entry.
• What does he or she look like?
• How does he or she act?
• How does he or she treat other characters?
• How do the other characters treat him or her? ▶

3. Next, describe what you like or dislike about the character. ▶

4. Lastly, talk to the character. Write what you might say to the character based on what he or she is like. ▶

UNIT 3 From Mystery to Medicine • **Lesson 3** *The Bridge Dancers*

▶ **Writing in a Literature Response Journal**

Journal Entry 3

Responding to a Plot

Write a response to the plot of the story you've chosen.
Answer some or all of the questions below and include them
in your journal entry. Support your opinions with examples
from the story and from your own experience. You can write
your journal entry on this page or in your Writer's Notebook.

1. Write today's date here. ▶

2. Write a response to the plot.
Include answers to some or all
of the following questions in
your journal entry.
• Do the problems the character
faces seem important or not?
• Does he or she solve the
problems in ways that make
sense?
• Did you think of better ways
to solve the problems as you
read the story? If so, what are
they?
• Does the ending seem real or
was the problem solved too
easily? What ending would have
made more sense to you?

► **Writing in a Literature Response Journal**

Journal Entry 4

Responding to the Writing

Respond to the way the author wrote the story or book you chose. Tell what you would keep and what you would change. Support your opinions and suggestions with examples and details from the story and from your own experience. Answer some or all of the questions below to help you write your entry. You can write your entry on this page or in your Writer's Notebook.

1. Write today's date here. ►

2. What do you think about the elements used in the story? Write your thoughts about the following elements here.
• the author's use of figurative language
• his or her use of dialogue
• the details the author uses to make the setting and characters seem real
►

3. Think about how you might change the story if you were the author. Would you
• use a different setting?
• delete or add a character?
• change something about the main character?
• change the problem the characters face in some way?
• add events to the plot?
►

Objective: Students practice writing in a literature response journal.

PERSONAL WRITING

Objective: Students prewrite a friendly letter.

Writing a Friendly Letter

Use the writing process to write a friendly letter.

Prewriting

Who is the *audience* for your letter?

☐ A friend who lives in another town or city

☐ A pen pal

☐ A relative your age

☐ Other _____

What is your *purpose* for writing?

☐ To tell a friend about something you've learned about medicine

☐ To tell a pen pal an interesting fact about medicine you read in an article

☐ To tell a cousin about "Emily's Hands-On Science Experiment"

☐ Other _____

Fill in information about the person to whom you are writing.

Person's name: _____

Street address: _____

City: _____ State: _____ Zip Code: _____

Name _____ Date _____

Objective: Students prewrite and draft a friendly letter.

PERSONAL WRITING

▶ Writing a Friendly Letter

Organize your friendly letter. Write your ideas on this page.

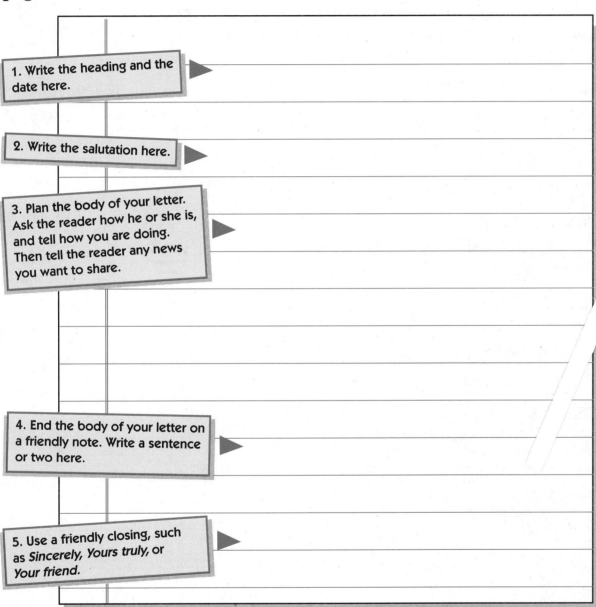

1. Write the heading and the date here.

2. Write the salutation here.

3. Plan the body of your letter. Ask the reader how he or she is, and tell how you are doing. Then tell the reader any news you want to share.

4. End the body of your letter on a friendly note. Write a sentence or two here.

5. Use a friendly closing, such as *Sincerely, Yours truly,* or *Your friend.*

Drafting

Write the first draft of your letter, in cursive. Write in complete sentences and include all the parts of a friendly letter.

Objective: Students revise a friendly letter.

▶ **Writing a Friendly Letter**

Revising

Read your personal letter carefully. Use this checklist to make your ideas clearer, and show any needed changes with proofreading marks.

Ideas

☐ Do you describe events that will interest your reader?

☐ Do you express concern about and interest in your reader?

Organization

☐ Are all the parts of a friendly letter included and in the correct places?

Word Choice

☐ Do you use words that your reader will understand?

Sentence Fluency

☐ Do you ask questions to add variety to your letter?

Voice

☐ Have you thought about how your letter will affect your reader?

☐ Does your letter share your excitement about something?

☐ Other _____

If you have made many changes, rewrite your letter on loose-leaf paper or on a computer. Keep a copy in your Writing Folder.

	Proofreading Marks
¶	Indent.
∧	Add something.
ℓ	Take something out.
∼	Transpose.
≡	Make a capital letter.
/	Make a small letter.
⌇	Check spelling.
⌒	Close up space.
#	Add space.
⊙	Add a period.

Objective: Students edit, proofread, and publish a friendly letter.

▶ **Writing a Friendly Letter**

Editing/Proofreading

Be sure to proofread your letter. Show that you care enough about the reader to correct your mistakes.

Conventions

☐ Make sure your pronouns agree with their antecedents.

☐ Check to see if you used commas correctly in your address, after the salutation, and after the closing.

☐ Review your other punctuation.

☐ Check your spelling and capitalization of names and other proper nouns.

☐ Other _____

Publishing

Use this checklist to get your letter ready to mail.

☐ Make sure your letter is neatly written or typed.

☐ Sign your first name. Include your last name only if the reader will be confused.

☐ Address the envelope. Proofread your spelling and punctuation.

☐ Fold your letter carefully and put it into the envelope. Add a stamp and mail it.

☐ Other _____

PERSONAL WRITING

Name _____ Date _____

Writing Notes and Cards: Invitations

Practice writing an invitation.

Read the following information. Then complete the invitation below based on the information.

Megan Ryan wants to give a birthday party for her younger sister, Brianna. Brianna's birthday is Saturday, December 9. Megan wants to give the party on the same day. The party will be at their house, 1167 North Avenue. Megan thinks a good time to start is 2:00 p.m. She also wants the guests to let her know if they plan to attend by calling her at home. Her home phone number is 784-1763.

You're invited to: _____ !

For: _____

Given by: _____

When: _____

Where: _____

_____

Time: _____

RSVP: _____

_____

Writing Notes and Cards: Thank-You Notes

Practice writing a thank-you note.

Think of a gift or an act of kindness you received from someone. In the space below or on another sheet of paper, draft a thank-you note to that person.

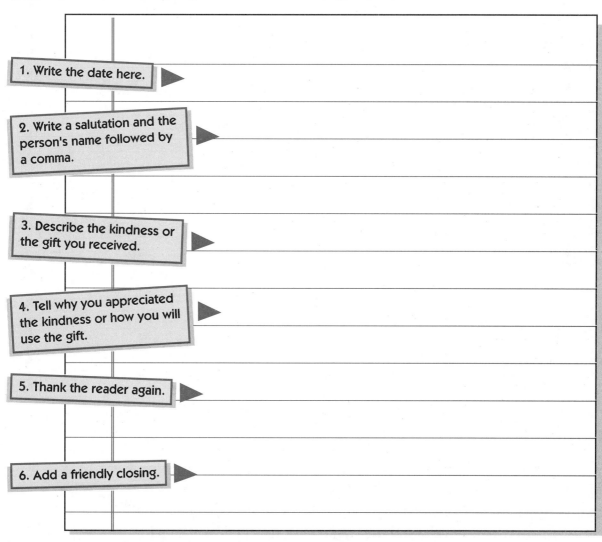

1. Write the date here.

2. Write a salutation and the person's name followed by a comma.

3. Describe the kindness or the gift you received.

4. Tell why you appreciated the kindness or how you will use the gift.

5. Thank the reader again.

6. Add a friendly closing.

Revise, proofread, and edit your thank-you note. Look for usage, punctuation, spelling, grammar, and other errors. Rewrite your note, making any necessary corrections, and mail it.

PERSONAL WRITING

Name _____ Date _____

Writing Notes and Cards: Get-Well Cards

Objective: Students practice writing a greeting in a get-well card.

Practice writing a note in a get-well card.

In the space below, draft a note you might write in a get-well card.

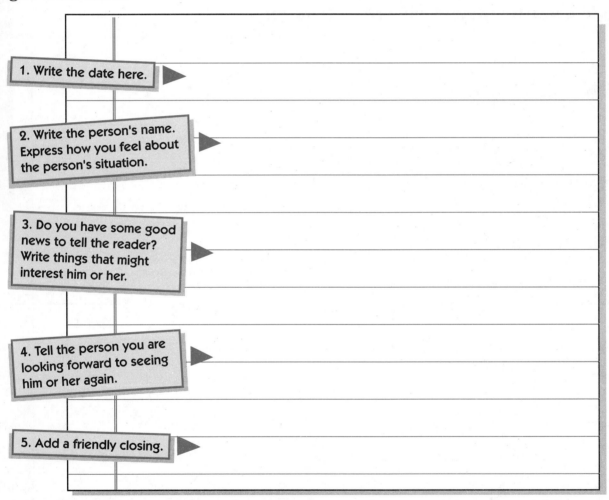

1. Write the date here.

2. Write the person's name. Express how you feel about the person's situation.

3. Do you have some good news to tell the reader? Write things that might interest him or her.

4. Tell the person you are looking forward to seeing him or her again.

5. Add a friendly closing.

Revise, edit, and proofread your note for spelling, usage, and other errors. Next, write it neatly in a blank get-well card that you made or bought and mail it.

Name _____ Date _____

Writing Notes and Cards: Phone Messages

PERSONAL WRITING

Read the following phone conversation. Imagine you received this call 12:30 p.m. on Wednesday, January 17. Write the message you would leave for your older brother, Steven, in the space below.

Caller: Hello! Is Steven there?

You: Not right now. Can I take a message?

Caller: Sure. Tell him to meet me at the school tonight so we can sit together at the basketball game, OK?

You: Who is this, please?

Caller: This is Jennifer Williams. I'm Steven's classmate.

You: What time did you want to meet?

Caller: About 7:15 p.m. would be good.

You: Where should he meet you at the school?

Caller: Oh, outside the front gym doors, I guess.

You: Jennifer, can you give me your telephone number?

Caller: Sure. It's 895-8240. He doesn't have to call me back, though.

You: I'll give him the message, Jennifer. Thanks for calling!

Telephone Message

For: _____

Date: _____

Time: _____

Caller: _____

Message: _____

_____

Call taken by: _____

Name _____ Date _____

Writing in a Learning Log

Practice writing a learning log.

Learning Log Entry 1

Making Observations

Gather information about the experiment you chose. In the space below or in your Writer's Notebook, write about the steps in the experiment as if you were watching it being performed.

1. Write the date here.

2. What medical experiment will you record?

3. Tell how the scientist or doctor did the experiment (cause). Write the steps.

4. Tell about the results of the experiment (effect).

PERSONAL WRITING

Objective: Students practice writing in a learning log.

▶ Writing in a Learning Log

Learning Log Entry 2

Using Prior Knowledge

What do you already know about the experiment you've chosen? Based on your prior knowledge, write questions and answers about the experiment in the space below or in your Writer's Notebook.

1. Write the date here. ▶

2. Write a question about the type of experiment. ▶

Write the answer to your first question here. ▶

3. Write a question about the steps of the experiment. ▶

Write the answer to your second question here. ▶

4. Write a question about the results of the experiment. ▶

Write the answer to your third question here. ▶

Objective: Students practice writing in a learning log.

Writing in a Learning Log

Learning Log Entry 3

Making Connections

Write about a subject or content area that relates to your experiment and to medicine. Then describe how the results of the experiment you've chosen might be used in that content area. Write your response in the space below or in your Writer's Notebook.

1. Write the date here.

2. Write a content area that relates to the experiment you've chosen and to medicine.

3. Write about how the content area relates to medicine.

4. Describe how the results of the medical experiment can be used in the subject area you've chosen.

Objective: Students practice writing in a learning log.

▶ **Writing in a Learning Log**

Learning Log Entry 4

Drawing Conclusions and Making Reflections

Think about everything you've learned about the experiment. Summarize it by drawing conclusions, making some personal reflections, and looking ahead. You can write in the space below or in your Writer's Notebook.

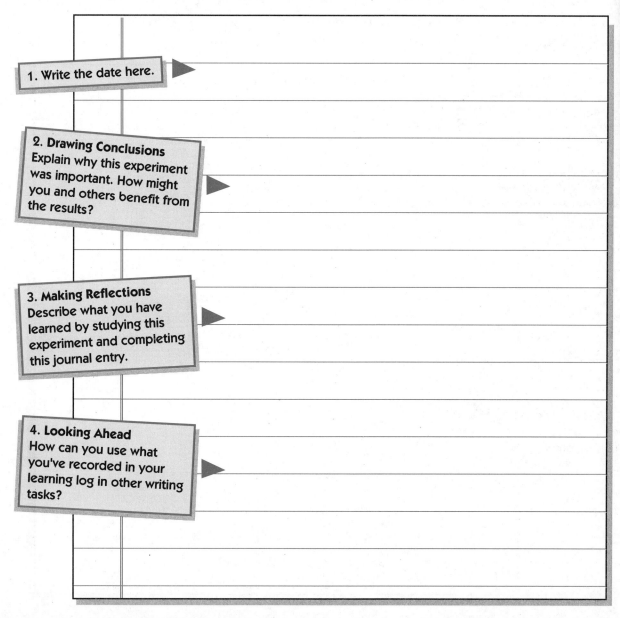

1. Write the date here. ▶

2. Drawing Conclusions Explain why this experiment was important. How might you and others benefit from the results? ▶

3. Making Reflections Describe what you have learned by studying this experiment and completing this journal entry. ▶

4. Looking Ahead How can you use what you've recorded in your learning log in other writing tasks? ▶

Writing in a Dialogue Journal

Objective: Students practice writing in a dialogue journal.

Practice writing in a dialogue journal.

Dialogue Journal Entry 1

Writing to a Teacher

In the space below, write to your teacher about an idea or question you have about medicine. Share some of your thoughts or find out what the teacher thinks about your idea or question.

1. Write today's date here.

2. Write your idea or question to the teacher.

3. To the teacher: Write your response to the student's idea or question here.

UNIT 3 From Mystery to Medicine • **Lesson 7** *Shadow of a Bull*

Objective: Students practice writing in a dialogue journal.

PERSONAL WRITING

Dialogue Journal Entry 2

Writing and Responding to a Classmate

Write a journal entry to a classmate. Use the topic you selected on Day 1 or another one related to the unit theme, From Mystery to Medicine. Describe your thoughts about the topic, ask your classmate a question about it, or talk about a report you might write about it. You might state an opinion and ask if your partner agrees with you. Then, switch journals with your classmate and write a response to him or her.

1. Write today's date here.

2. Write your idea or question to your classmate here.

3. To the classmate: Read the entry above and respond to it. Respond to your partner's idea or question and share your thoughts and opinions about it. Write your response in the space below.

▶ **Writing in a Dialogue Journal**

Dialogue Journal Entry 3

Responding to a Teacher

Read and think about your teacher's response to the journal entry you wrote to him or her. Then write your response to your teacher on the same page or in the space below. Answer any questions in your teacher's response and explain the reasons for your answer. Share your ideas and thoughts, just as you would in a conversation.

1. Write today's date here. ▶

2. Write your response to your teacher's comments or questions about your first journal entry. ▶

Objective: Students practice writing in a dialogue journal.

Writing in a Dialogue Journal

Dialogue Journal Entry 4

Summary

Reflect on the entries in your dialogue journal. Write about what you've learned from each journal entry. Then write how you might use what you've learned for other writing tasks. Write in the space below or in your Writer's Notebook.

1. Write the date here.

2. Write what you've learned from your journal entry to your teacher.

3. Write what you've learned from your journal entry to your classmate.

4. Tell how you can use at least one of these entries in a different writing task, such as a report, article, story, or poem.

Objective: Students practice writing in a dialogue journal.

PERSONAL WRITING

Writing a Personal Narrative

Objective: Students prewrite personal narratives.

Use the writing process to write a personal narrative.

Prewriting

Who is the audience for your personal narrative?

☐ Your teacher

☐ Classmates

☐ Readers of a children's magazine

☐ Other _____

What is your purpose for writing your personal narrative?

☐ To tell how you solved a problem

☐ To tell about how you dealt with something that concerned you

☐ To tell a funny story about how you solved a specific problem

☐ Other _____

Writing a Personal Narrative

NARRATIVE WRITING

Objective: Students prewrite personal narratives.

Fill in the problem-resolution graphic organizer to help you organize the details of a problem you had and how you solved it.

Problem:

↓

Actions to Solve the Problem:

↓

Resolution:

Drafting

Write the first draft of your personal narrative on loose-leaf paper or a computer. Refer to your graphic organizer to make sure you stay on topic. Keep a copy of your draft in your Writing Folder.

UNIT 4 Survival • **Lesson I** *Island of the Blue Dolphins*

▶ **Writing a Personal Narrative**

Objective: Students revise personal narratives.

Revising

Read the draft of your personal narrative. Then follow this checklist to improve your writing. Use proofreading marks as you make changes.

Ideas

☐ Will your personal narrative make sense to your readers?

☐ Do you use details to make your narrative interesting?

Organization

☐ Does each paragraph contain a topic sentence and sentences with details that support the topic sentence?

☐ Do you use transition words in your sentences and paragraphs to show how your ideas are organized in your narrative?

Word Choice

☐ Do you use a variety of words and phrases instead of saying the same thing over and over?

Sentence Fluency

☐ Do you use some simple, compound, and complex sentences in your narrative for variety?

Voice

☐ Does your narrative sound like you wrote it?

☐ Does the tone of the writing fit your purpose and audience?

☐ Other _____

Proofreading Marks	
	Indent.
	Add something.
	Take something out.
	Transpose.
	Make a capital letter.
	Make a small letter.
	Check spelling.
	Close up space.
	Add space.
	Add a period.

Make sure you've marked everything that needs changing. Then rewrite your personal narrative by hand or on a computer, making all revisions.

NARRATIVE WRITING

Writing a Personal Narrative

Editing/Proofreading

It is important to proofread your revised draft. Use this checklist to make sure you remember to check everything.

Conventions

☐ Make sure that all words are correctly spelled, even if you used a computer spell checker. You can also use spelling strategies or a dictionary to check your spelling.

☐ Check all punctuation to make sure that it is correct.

☐ Make sure that each sentence and all proper nouns begin with a capital letter.

☐ Make sure that comparative and superlative adjectives are formed correctly.

☐ Read your narrative aloud to help correct grammar errors such as fragments and run-on sentences.

☐ Other _____

Publishing

Use this checklist to get your personal narrative ready for publication.

Presentation

☐ If working on a computer, print a final copy. If handwriting, write a neat final copy.

☐ Include illustrations or photographs. Present them neatly by pasting them onto a sheet of paper or by scanning and placing them in your electronic file.

☐ Send your narrative to a newspaper or magazine for possible publication. Make sure that you have followed the publication's rules for preparing your writing for publication.

UNIT 4 Survival • **Lesson 2** *Arctic Explorer: The Story of Matthew Henson*

Writing a Realistic Story

Use the writing process to write a realistic story.

Prewriting

Who is the audience for your story?

☐ Classmates

☐ Younger children

☐ Other _____

What is your purpose for writing this realistic story?

☐ To tell an entertaining story that gives information about a particular country or region

☐ To tell an entertaining story about an adventurer who travels to a jungle or desert

☐ Other _____

Answer these questions before you begin writing.

Who are the main characters in your story? _____

_____

What is the problem that the main characters face?

_____

_____

What is the setting of your story? _____

_____

Name _____ Date _____

▶ **Writing a Realistic Story**

Objective: Students prewrite and draft realistic stories.

Fill in the story map graphic organizer to organize your ideas for your realistic story.

Title:

Characters:

Setting:

Plot (What Happened):

Beginning (Problem): _____

Middle (Events):

1. _____

2. _____

3. _____

Ending (How the problem was solved):

_____

_____

Drafting

Write a draft of your realistic story on loose-leaf paper or a computer. Refer to your story map as you write. Keep a copy of your draft in your Writing Folder.

NARRATIVE WRITING

UNIT 4 Survival • **Lesson 2** *Arctic Explorer: The Story of Matthew Henson*

Objective: Students revise realistic stories.

▶ **Writing a Realistic Story**

Revising

Read your draft. Use this checklist to make your story better. Use proofreading marks as you make changes.

Ideas

☐ Do your characters seem like real people?

☐ Do you include details about setting and action that will interest your audience?

Organization

☐ Does the action in the story move forward?

☐ Does your story have a clear beginning, middle, and ending?

Word Choice

☐ Do you use precise nouns, verbs, adjectives, and adverbs to bring the characters and setting to life?

Sentence Fluency

☐ Do you vary the beginnings of some of your sentences?

☐ Do you use transition words to help readers make connections between ideas in sentences and paragraphs?

Voice

☐ Does your story sound like you wrote it?

☐ Other _____

Read through your revisions one last time to make sure you changed everything that you want to. Then create a new copy of your story to put in your Writing Folder, making all revisions.

Proofreading Marks

¶	Indent.
∧	Add something.
℮	Take something out.
∼	Transpose.
≡	Make a capital letter.
/	Make a small letter.
⌇	Check spelling.
⊃⊂	Close up space.
#	Add space.
⊙	Add a period.

▶ **Writing a Realistic Story**

Editing/Proofreading

Edit and proofread your revised draft. Your final copy should be error-free. Use this checklist as you make final changes to your story.

Conventions

☐ Make sure that all words are correctly spelled, even if you used a computer spell checker. You can also use spelling strategies or a dictionary to check your spelling.

☐ Check all punctuation to make sure that it is correct.

☐ Make sure that each sentence and proper noun begins with a capital letter.

☐ Read your story aloud to catch grammar errors such as sentence fragments and run-on sentences.

☐ Other _____

Publishing

Use this checklist to get your realistic story ready for publication for your teacher, a school newspaper, or a class story collection.

Presentation

☐ If you are writing by hand, write a neat final copy.

☐ If you are working on a computer, print a final copy.

☐ Read your work one more time. Correct any errors.

☐ You can bind your work into a book and keep a copy in your classroom for others to read.

☐ Read your story aloud to your classmates or to younger students.

NARRATIVE WRITING

UNIT 4 Survival • **Lesson 3** *McBroom and the Big Wind*

Writing a Tall Tale

Objective: Students prewrite tall tales.

Use the writing process to write a tall tale.

Prewriting

Who is the audience for your tall tale?

☐ Your teacher

☐ Your classmates

☐ Younger children

☐ Other _____

What is your purpose?

☐ To share a humorous story about a made-up character

☐ To create a humorous story about a traditional tall-tale character

☐ To create a funny tale based on something you have experienced or know

☐ Other _____

On the lines below, write the ways that you might exaggerate the weather that will be part of your setting, the main characters and what they do and say, and the events in the story.

_____

_____

_____

_____

_____

▶ **Writing a Tall Tale**

NARRATIVE WRITING

Organize your tall tale using a plot line graphic organizer. Write the main characters, setting, problem, events, climax, and solution in the spaces provided.

Climax

_____

_____

_____

Write the events that happen in the middle of your tall tale on these lines.

_____

_____

Characters _____

_____

Setting _____

_____

Problem _____

_____

End of problem or conflict

_____

_____

_____

Drafting

Write the first draft of your tall tale on loose-leaf paper or on a computer. Follow your plot line graphic organizer as you write your draft. Keep a copy of your writing in your Writing Folder.

UNIT 4 Survival • **Lesson 3** *McBroom and the Big Wind*

Objective: Students revise tall tales.

▶ **Writing a Tall Tale**

Revising

Use this checklist to improve your writing. Use proofreading marks as you make changes.

Ideas

☐ Do you effectively use exaggeration to create humor?

☐ Do the events in your tall tale build to a climax?

Organization

☐ Does your story have a beginning, a middle, and an end?

Word Choice

☐ Have you used the right adjectives and adverbs to make your exaggerations funny?

Sentence Fluency

☐ Are your sentences varied in terms of length and structure?

☐ Do you vary the beginnings of your sentences?

☐ Do you use transition words to connect ideas in sentences and paragraphs?

Voice

☐ Does your sense of humor show in your tall tale?

☐ Other _____

Proofreading Marks	
¶	Indent.
∧	Add something.
ℯ	Take something out.
∼	Transpose.
≡	Make a capital letter.
/	Make a small letter.
⌀	Check spelling.
⊂⊃	Close up space.
#	Add space.
⊙	Add a period.

Correct everything that needs changing, and rewrite your tall tale by hand or on a computer.

▶ **Writing a Tall Tale**

(sidebar, vertical text) Objective: Students edit, proofread, and publish tall tales.

(sidebar, vertical text) **NARRATIVE WRITING**

Editing/Proofreading

It is important to proofread your revised draft. Don't let your readers be distracted by mistakes. Use this checklist to make sure that you remember to check everything.

Conventions

☐ Check all words for correct spelling, even if you used a computer spell checker. You can also use spelling strategies or a dictionary to check your spelling.

☐ Check all punctuation to make sure that it is correct.

☐ Make sure that each sentence begins with a capital letter. Also, all proper nouns should begin with a capital letter.

☐ Read your tall tale aloud to a classmate. Listen for grammar errors such as run-on sentences, misplaced modifiers, and sentence fragments.

☐ Other _____

Publishing

Use this checklist to prepare your tall tale for publication.

Presentation

☐ If working on a computer, print a final copy. If writing by hand, neatly write a final copy.

☐ Read your work one more time. Neatly correct any errors.

☐ Include illustrations or use clip art from the computer.

☐ Make a collection of tall tales. Bind your tall tale in a book with those of your classmates.

UNIT 4   Survival • **Lesson 4** *The Big Wave*

Writing a Fable

Use the writing process to write a fable.

Prewriting

Who is the audience for your fable?

☐ Other students in your school

☐ Your teacher

☐ Your parent

☐ Other _____

What is your purpose?

☐ To tell a story that teaches a lesson you've learned

☐ To share with your audience a lesson you think is important

☐ Other _____

In the space below, write a moral you might use for your fable. You can get ideas from fables you have read. Then write the lesson about life that the moral teaches.

What is the moral of your fable?

_____

_____

_____

What is the lesson about life that the moral teaches?

_____

_____

Objective: Students prewrite fables.

UNIT 4 Survival • **Lesson 4** *The Big Wave*

▶ **Writing a Fable**

Fill in the story map to help you organize your ideas for the characters, plot, and setting of your fable. As you plan, think about how the events will support the moral of your fable.

Objective: Students prewrite and draft fables.

NARRATIVE WRITING

Beginning

↓

Middle

↓

End

Drafting

Write the first draft of your fable on loose-leaf paper or a computer. Refer to your story map to stay on track as you draft. Keep a copy of your writing in your Writing Folder.

Objective: Students revise their fables.

▶ **Writing a Fable**

Revising

Use this checklist to improve your writing. Use proofreading marks to make any changes.

Ideas

☐ Do your characters and the way they act fit the fable?

☐ Does your fable stay focused on the moral?

Organization

☐ Does your fable have a beginning, a middle, and an end?

Word Choice

☐ Did you use the best words, or are there better words to express your thoughts?

Sentence Fluency

☐ Do most of your sentences sound the same, or is there variety among them?

☐ Do you use transition words to connect ideas in your sentences?

Voice

☐ Does the overall mood of the fable match the fable's moral?

☐ Other _____

Create a new copy of your fable by hand or on a computer, making all revisions.

Proofreading Marks

	Indent.
∧	Add something.
	Take something out.
∼	Transpose.
≡	Make a capital letter.
/	Make a small letter.
	Check spelling.
⊃⊂	Close up space.
∧#	Add space.
⊙	Add a period.

▶ **Writing a Fable**

NARRATIVE WRITING

Editing/Proofreading

Editing and proofreading your work carefully is important. Don't let your readers be distracted by mistakes. Use this checklist to make sure that you remember to check everything.

Conventions

☐ Make sure that all words are spelled correctly, even if you used a computer spell checker.

☐ Check all punctuation to make sure it is correct.

☐ Make sure that each sentence and all proper nouns begin with a capital letter.

☐ Look for sentence fragments, run-on sentences, and misplaced modifiers.

☐ Other _____

Publishing

Use this checklist to get your fable ready for publication. Here are some publishing options.

Presentation

☐ Illustrate and bind your fable as if it were a picture book for younger children.

☐ Bind your fable with those of your classmates to create a class fable collection.

☐ Print out or write a neat final copy.

☐ Read your work one more time to make sure there are no errors in the final copy.

☐ Create one or more illustrations for your fable.

☐ Make an attractive cover sheet or title page, or follow your teacher's instructions for including your fable in a class collection.

Writing a Biography

Use the writing process to write a biography.

Prewriting

Who is the audience for your biography?

☐ Your teacher

☐ Other students interested in the subject of your biography

☐ Your own and your classmates' parents

☐ Other _____

What is your purpose?

☐ To share the courageous experiences of a real-life person

☐ To tell a true story about someone who is a survivor

☐ Other _____

Use the space below to write down information about the person you chose.

Person's name _____

Birthdate _____

Birthplace _____

This person is worth writing about because _____

_____

_____

_____

UNIT 4 Survival • **Lesson 5** *Anne Frank: Diary of a Young Girl*

Writing a Biography

NARRATIVE WRITING

Organize the information about the subject of your biography using the time line below. Write the events or the subject's accomplishments that you will include in your biography in the boxes. Make sure that you write the events and accomplishments in time, or chronological, order.

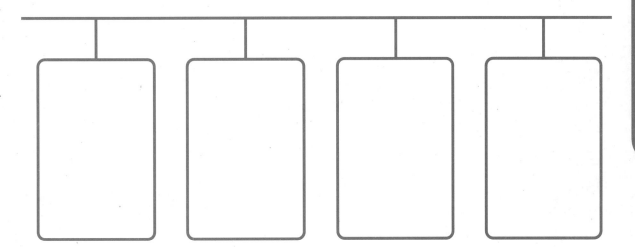

Drafting

Write the first draft of your biography on loose-leaf paper or on a computer. Refer to your time line to make sure you present events in time order.

UNIT 4 Survival • **Lesson 5** *Anne Frank: Diary of a Young Girl*

▶ **Writing a Biography**

Revising

Read the draft of your biography. Use the checklist to improve your draft. Use proofreading marks to make changes.

Ideas

☐ Do you clearly tell the important parts of your subject's life?

☐ Do you include details that will interest your specific audience?

Organization

☐ Are the events in the subject's life presented clearly in time order?

☐ Do you use a variety of signal words to show relationships between events?

Word Choice

☐ Do your words describe your subject in a way that tells the readers how the person really is/was?

Sentence Fluency

☐ Do you vary the beginnings of your sentences?

☐ Do you use a variety of sentence structures so that your sentences don't all sound the same?

Voice

☐ Does your biography sound too much like the sources you used?

☐ Other _____

Proofreading Marks	
¶	Indent.
∧	Add something.
℮	Take something out.
∼	Transpose.
≡	Make a capital letter.
/	Make a small letter.
⟲	Check spelling.
⌒	Close up space.
#	Add space.
⊙	Add a period.

Read your revised work aloud to make sure you caught everything that needs changing. Then rewrite your biography by hand or on a computer.

▶ **Writing a Biography**

Objective: Students edit, proofread, and publish biographies.

NARRATIVE WRITING

Editing/Proofreading

Use this checklist to make sure you remember to check everything. Work with a peer reviewer so that you can proofread each other's writing.

Conventions

☐ Make sure that all words are correctly spelled, even if you used a computer spell checker. You can also use spelling strategies or a dictionary to check your spelling.

☐ Check all punctuation to make sure it is correct.

☐ Make sure that each sentence begins with a capital letter.

☐ Make sure that all proper nouns begin with a capital letter.

☐ Check for sentence fragments and run-on sentences.

☐ Other _____

Publishing

Use this checklist to get your biography ready for publication. The following are some publishing options:

Presentation

☐ Submit your biography to a magazine whose readers would be interested in the subject.

☐ Submit your biography to a Web site that accepts student work of this type.

☐ Print out or write a final copy on clean paper. If you are going to submit your work to a Web site, double-check that your electronic copy is correct.

☐ Read your biography one more time to make sure that you didn't create any new errors in the final copy.

☐ If you are going to submit the biography to a magazine or Web site, find out exactly what format the editor or publisher requires.

Writing a Play

Use the writing process to write a play.

Prewriting

Who is the audience for your play?

☐ Your class

☐ Other students in your school

☐ Parents or other grown-ups

☐ Other _____

What is your purpose?

☐ To perform a story based on the songs of African slaves

☐ To share a story of survival or bravery

☐ Other _____

In the space below, write your ideas for your play.

Characters: _____

_____

Setting: _____

_____

What story will your play tell? _____

_____

Name _____ Date _____

▶ **Writing a Play**

Plan and organize your play on this page.

Setting

Characters

Plot

Scenes and Stage Directions

Dialogue

Drafting

Write the first draft of your play on loose-leaf paper or on a computer. Use your prewriting plans as a guide. Keep a copy of your draft in your Writing Folder.

Objective: Students prewrite and draft plays.

NARRATIVE WRITING

UNIT 4 Survival • **Lesson 6** *Music and Slavery*

Objective: Students revise plays.

► **Writing a Play**

Revising

Read the draft of your play silently or to a classmate. Use this checklist to improve your work. Use proofreading marks as you make changes.

Ideas
☐ Does your dialogue keep the story moving?
☐ Do your characters seem like real people?

Organization
☐ Is the interaction among your characters realistic?
☐ Is the format of your play correct?

Word Choice
☐ Do your characters say things that people might really say?
☐ Do your characters use words that the audience will understand?

Voice
☐ Does your play sound like you wrote it?

☐ Other _____

Read your revisions to make sure that you have marked everything that needs changing. Then, create a new copy of your play by hand or on a computer, making all revisions.

Proofreading Marks

¶	Indent.
∧	Add something.
ℓ	Take something out.
∼	Transpose.
≡	Make a capital letter.
/	Make a small letter.
⊷	Check spelling.
⌒	Close up space.
#	Add space.
⊙	Add a period.

UNIT 4 Survival • **Lesson 6** *Music and Slavery*

> **Writing a Play**

Editing/Proofreading

Don't let your audience be distracted by mistakes. Use this checklist to make sure you check everything.

Conventions

☐ Make sure that all words are correctly spelled, even if you used a computer spell checker. You can also use spelling strategies or a dictionary to check your spelling.

☐ Check all punctuation to make sure it is correct.

☐ Make sure that each sentence and proper noun begins with a capital letter.

☐ Look for and correct any grammar errors such as sentence fragments, run-on sentences, and misplaced modifiers.

☐ Other _____

Publishing

Use this checklist to get your play ready for publication. Publishing a play can mean allowing people to read it, or it can mean having actors perform the play. Either way, your audience needs a neat, clean copy.

Presentation

☐ If working on a computer, print a final copy.

☐ If writing by hand, write a neat copy.

☐ Read your work one more time. Correct any errors that you made in the final copy.

☐ Perform your play before an audience of your classmates or younger students.

☐ If you are directing, make sure all actors speak clearly and loudly enough for everyone in the audience to understand.

UNIT 5 Communication • **Lesson I** *Messages by the Mile*

Persuasive Paragraph

Use the writing process to organize and write a
persuasive paragraph.

Prewriting

Who is the audience for your paragraph?

☐ Your teacher

☐ An adult in your family

☐ A child in your family

☐ A friend

☐ Classmates

☐ Other _____

What is your purpose for writing?

☐ To persuade readers that some animals "speak" to humans

☐ To persuade readers that certain animals communicate
with each other

☐ Other _____

**Write some ideas about animal communication that you
might want to include in your paragraph.**

_____

_____

_____

_____

_____

Name _____ Date _____

Objective: Students prewrite and draft their persuasive paragraphs.

►**Persuasive Paragraph**

Use this main idea web to organize your ideas for your
persuasive paragraph. Write your main idea in the
center circle. Then write the subtopics you might
include on the long lines. Put details about each
subtopic on the shorter lines.

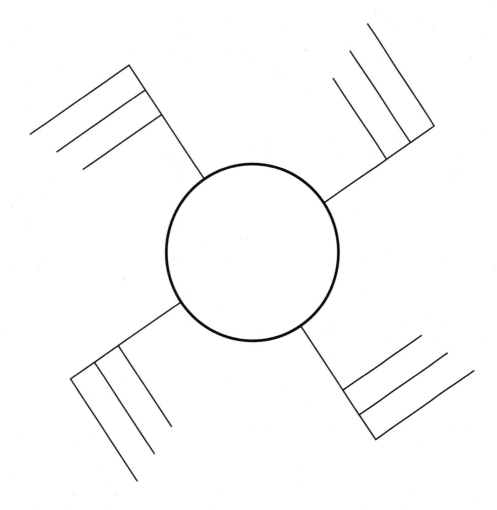

Drafting

Write the first draft of your paragraph on loose-leaf
paper or on a computer. Follow your prewriting plan
and keep a copy of your draft in your Writing Folder.

PERSUASIVE WRITING

► **Persuasive Paragraph**

Objective: Students revise their paragraphs.

Revising

Read your paragraph carefully. Use this checklist to make it clearer, and use proofreading marks to show any changes.

Ideas

☐ Is your opinion clearly explained?

☐ Did you include facts or an emotional appeal to support your opinion?

Organization

☐ Does your topic sentence express your opinion?

☐ Have you put your facts or examples in order from weakest to strongest?

☐ Does your last sentence repeat your opinion, using different words?

Word Choice

☐ Did you use specific and precise words?

Sentence Fluency

☐ When you read your paragraph aloud, are there any awkward sentences?

Voice

☐ Does your paragraph show that you support what you say?

☐ Other _____

Proofreading Marks	
¶	Indent.
∧	Add something.
℮	Take something out.
∼	Transpose.
≡	Make a capital letter.
/	Make a small letter.
⬭	Check spelling.
⊂	Close up space.
#	Add space.
⊙	Add a period.

If you have made many changes, rewrite your revised version by hand, writing in cursive, or on a computer.

▶ **Persuasive Paragraph**

Editing/Proofreading

Be sure to proofread your paragraph. Make sure it is as clear and convincing as possible. Don't let readers become distracted by mistakes in spelling or grammar.

Conventions

☐ Did you include different kinds of phrases in your paragraph?

☐ Did you separate appositives and participial phrases from the sentence with commas?

☐ Is your other punctuation correct?

☐ Does each sentence and proper noun begin with a capital letter?

☐ Did you check your spelling, even if you used a computer spell checker?

☐ Other _____

Publishing

Use this checklist to get your paragraph ready for readers.

Presentation

☐ Make a neat copy by hand or on a computer.

☐ Check to see if you indented the paragraph.

☐ Think of several ways to share your paragraph with people outside the classroom. For example, you could send it to the school or community newspaper or e-mail it to someone who is interested in your topic.

☐ Other _____

PERSUASIVE WRITING

Name _____ Date _____

Writing an Advertisement

Use the writing process to plan and write an advertisement for your peers.

Prewriting

Who is the audience for your ad?

☐ Classmates

☐ Other students at school

☐ Other young people in the community

☐ Other _____

What is your purpose for writing an ad?

☐ To persuade readers to think about your product or service in a certain way

☐ To convince readers to buy your product or service

☐ To entertain readers

☐ Other _____

What product or service are you going to advertise? How will you advertise it? Write your ideas here.

_____

_____

_____

_____

_____

UNIT 5 Communication • **Lesson 2** *We'll Be Right Back After These Messages*

▶ **Writing an Advertisement**

One way to convince readers to buy a product or service is to show a cause and effect relationship. Use the cause-and-effect map below to organize your ideas for your advertisement.

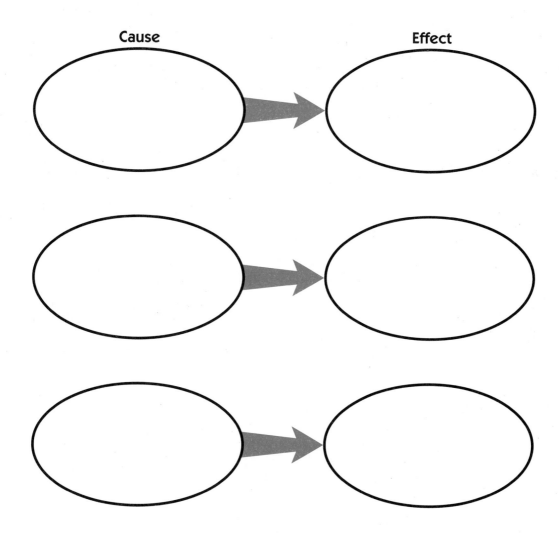

Cause   Effect

Drafting

Write a draft of your ad on loose-leaf paper or on a computer. Because this is an ad, you can express some of your ideas in words or phrases instead of complete sentences. Sketch your ideas for an illustration that might go with the words in your ad.

Objective: Students prewrite and draft their advertisements.

PERSUASIVE WRITING

UNIT 5 Communication • **Lesson 2** *We'll Be Right Back After These Messages*

▶ **Writing an Advertisement**

Objective: Students revise their advertisements.

Revising

Read your ad carefully. Use this checklist to make sure it is as convincing as possible. Show any needed changes with proofreading marks.

Ideas

☐ Did you give the most convincing reasons to buy your product or service?

Organization

☐ Did you arrange your words and illustrations to grab the readers' attention?

Word Choice

☐ Did you use words that your audience will understand and relate to?

☐ Did you eliminate any unnecessary words?

Sentence Fluency

☐ Did you use words or phrases instead of sentences in some places?

Voice

☐ Did you focus your ad on the needs of your audience?

☐ Is your ad full of energy and excitement?

☐ Are readers likely to read your ad and say! "Yes! I need that!"?

☐ Other _____

Mark all the needed changes. Rewrite your revised version by hand or on a computer.

	Proofreading Marks
	Indent.
	Add something.
	Take something out.
	Transpose.
	Make a capital letter.
	Make a small letter.
	Check spelling.
	Close up space.
	Add space.
	Add a period.

> **Writing an Advertisement**

Editing/Proofreading

Be sure to proofread your ad. Mistakes can distract readers from your message. Use this checklist to find them.

Conventions

☐ Did you capitalize the first word of each sentence and each proper noun?

☐ Did you remember that, in an ad, you can use exclamation marks or no punctuation at the end of phrases?

☐ Are all words spelled correctly?

☐ Other _____

Publishing

Use this checklist to get your advertisement ready to sell your product or service.

Presentation

☐ Make sure your ad is interesting to look at and not too crowded. Create the illustration for your ad by hand or on a computer.

☐ Brainstorm several ways to make sure potential customers see your ad. For example, you might make it into a poster or a flyer. You could display the posters at school, with permission from school staff. You might hand flyers to your friends or take them door-to-door in your neighborhood. Perhaps your neighborhood has a newsletter that would print your ad.

☐ Choose your best publishing idea and carry it out.

☐ Other _____

PERSUASIVE WRITING

Objective: Students edit, proofread, and publish their advertisements.

UNIT 5 Communication • **Lesson 3** *Breaking into Print*

Writing a Letter to the Editor

Objective: Students prewrite their letters.

Use the writing process to write a letter to the editor.

Prewriting

Who is the audience for your letter?

☐ The editor of a newspaper: _____

☐ The editor of a magazine: _____

☐ Your family

☐ People in the community

☐ Other _____

What is your purpose for writing?

☐ To convince readers to share your opinion about a problem that was stated in a newspaper article

☐ To persuade an editor of a newspaper or magazine to print articles or letters about a specific problem in your community

☐ To persuade readers that a problem in your community should be solved in a certain way

☐ To state your opinion about another letter to the editor you read in a newspaper or magazine

☐ Other _____

▶ Writing a Letter to the Editor

Use the space below to organize the ideas for the body of your letter to the editor.

Write the problem or issue that concerns you:

_____

_____

Write your opinion about the problem or issue:

_____

_____

Write the reasons that support your opinion:

_____

_____

_____

Write why your readers should agree with your opinion:

_____

_____

_____

_____

_____

Drafting

Write a draft of your letter on loose-leaf paper or on a computer. Use the format for a business letter, including the heading, inside address, salutation, body, closing, and signature. The information in the body of your letter should be based on the information above.

Objective: Students prewrite and draft their letters.

PERSUASIVE WRITING

UNIT 5 Communication • **Lesson 3** *Breaking into Print*

Objective: Students revise their letters.

Revising

Read your letter carefully, answering the questions on this checklist. Use proofreading marks to show any needed changes.

Ideas

☐ Did you refer to the article in your letter?

☐ Did you support your opinion with facts and examples?

Organization

☐ Do you use the format of a business letter to organize your letter to the editor?

Word Choice

☐ Have you used specific, interesting words instead of general ones?

☐ Did you explain your ideas in a way that your whole audience (not just the editor) will understand?

Sentence Fluency

☐ Did you use sentences of different lengths that begin in different ways?

Voice

☐ Does your letter show that you have strong feelings about the problem or issue you address in your letter?

☐ Other _____

Rewrite your letter by hand or on a computer, making all necessary changes.

Proofreading Marks	
¶	Indent.
∧	Add something.
℮	Take something out.
~	Transpose.
≡	Make a capital letter.
/	Make a small letter.
sp	Check spelling.
) (	Close up space.
#	Add space.
⊙	Add a period.

Name ______________________ Date ____________

Writing a Letter to the Editor

PERSUASIVE WRITING

Objective: Students edit, proofread, and publish their letters.

Editing/Proofreading

Be sure to proofread your letter. You don't want to see your mistakes printed in a newspaper or magazine!

Conventions

- ☐ Did you spell the names of people and places correctly?
- ☐ Are all words spelled correctly?
- ☐ Does each sentence begin with a capital letter and end with the correct punctuation mark?
- ☐ Did you check the punctuation of the heading, inside address, salutation, and closing?
- ☐ Other ______________________

Publishing

Use this checklist to get your letter ready for your audience.

Presentation

- ☐ Make sure your writing or typing is neat, with no crossed-out words or other mistakes.
- ☐ Fold your letter correctly and put it in an envelope.
- ☐ Carefully address the envelope to the editor of the school or community newspaper or the magazine you have chosen.
- ☐ Add a stamp and mail it.
- ☐ Other ______________________

Writing a Persuasive Report for Peers

Objective: Student prewrite persuasive reports.

Use the writing process to organize and write a persuasive report for your peers.

Prewriting

Who is the audience for your report?

☐ Your classmates

☐ A friend

☐ Other young people your age: _____

☐ Other _____

What is your purpose for writing?

☐ To persuade readers that primates communicate in a manner similar to humans.

☐ To persuade readers that dolphins communicate in a manner similar to humans.

☐ Other _____

What is your opinion about communication?

What two ideas about communication will you compare and contrast in your report?

_____

_____

_____

_____

UNIT 5 Communication • **Lesson 4** *Koko's Kitten*

Writing a Persuasive Report for Peers

PERSUASIVE WRITING

Use this Venn diagram to organize the details you will compare and contrast in your persuasive report.

Title: _____

Different   Alike   Different

Drafting

Write the draft of your report on loose-leaf paper in cursive or on a computer, following your prewriting plans. Keep a copy of your draft in your Writing Folder.

UNIT 5 Communication • **Lesson 4** *Koko's Kitten*

Objective: Students revise their reports.

Revising

▶ **Writing a Persuasive Report for Peers**

Read your report carefully. Use this checklist to make it as persuasive as possible. Show any needed changes with proofreading marks.

Ideas

☐ Is your opinion clearly stated?

☐ Have you included facts and details or an emotional appeal to support your opinion?

☐ Have you answered any reasons that readers might have for rejecting your opinion?

Organization

☐ Did you begin by explaining your opinion?

☐ Have you put your points in order from weakest to strongest?

☐ Did you end by restating your opinion?

Word Choice

☐ Did you include words that are specific and precise, so readers will understand your ideas?

☐ Did you use words that are familiar to your readers?

Sentence Fluency

☐ Do you have a topic sentence?

☐ Do you use different kinds of sentences?

Voice

☐ Does your report show that you feel strongly about a problem or issue?

☐ Other _____

Rewrite revised version of your persuasive report on loose-leaf paper or on a computer.

Proofreading Marks	
¶	Indent.
∧	Add something.
ℯ	Take something out.
∼	Transpose.
≡	Make a capital letter.
/	Make a small letter.
⌇	Check spelling.
⊂⊃	Close up space.
#	Add space.
⊙	Add a period.

▶ Writing a Persuasive Report for Peers

Objective: Students edit, proofread, and publish their reports.

PERSUASIVE WRITING

Editing/Proofreading

Don't forget to proofread your report. You don't want careless mistakes to distract readers from your main points.

Conventions

☐ Did you write in complete sentences, avoiding fragments, run-on, rambling, or awkward sentences?

☐ Did you use correct punctuation?

☐ Are the first words of each sentence and any proper nouns capitalized?

☐ Did you check your spelling, even if you used a computer spell checker?

☐ Other _____

Publishing

Use this checklist to get your report ready for your classmates to read.

Presentation

☐ Write or type your report neatly and indent your paragraphs.

☐ Consider using bullets to make your points stand out.

☐ Consider adding a drawing or picture in your report.

☐ Think of several ways to share your report with others. For example, you and other group members can take turns reading your reports aloud.

☐ Other _____

Writing a Persuasive Report for Adults

Use the writing process to write a persuasive report for an audience of adults.

Prewriting

Who is the audience for your report?

☐ Your teacher

☐ Your family

☐ The school librarian or media specialist

☐ The PTA

☐ Other _____

What is your purpose for writing?

☐ To persuade readers to fix a problem

☐ To persuade readers to agree with your opinion

☐ To persuade readers to act a certain way concerning a problem or issue

☐ Other _____

▶ **Writing a Persuasive Report for Adults**

Use this problem/resolution chart to organize the ideas in your persuasive report. Write the problem in the space provided. Then list ways to solve the problem in order of importance.

Problem-Resolution Chart for _____

Problem:

↓

Actions to Solve Problem:

↓

Resolution:

Drafting

Write a draft of your report on loose-leaf paper in cursive or on a computer, following your prewriting plans. Keep a copy of your report in your Writing Folder.

Objective: Students prewrite and draft their reports.

PERSUASIVE WRITING

Revising

> **Writing a Persuasive Report for Adults**

Read your report carefully. Use this checklist to make it clearer and more convincing. Use proofreading marks to show any needed changes.

Ideas

☐ Did you clearly explain your recommended action—what you want the reader to do?

☐ Did you include facts and examples to support your request?

Organization

☐ Did you begin in a way that will interest adult readers?

☐ Did you order your points from weakest to strongest?

Word Choice

☐ Did you use words that are appropriate for adult readers?

Sentence Fluency

☐ Does each sentence lead to the next one, with no sudden jumps in topic?

☐ Does each paragraph lead smoothly to the next one?

Voice

☐ Will readers be able to tell that the issue or problem you write about is important to you?

☐ Other _____

Rewrite your report on loose-leaf paper or on a computer. Keep a copy in your Writing Folder.

Proofreading Marks

 Indent.

 Add something.

 Take something out.

 Transpose.

 Make a capital letter.

 Make a small letter.

 Check spelling.

 Close up space.

 Add space.

⊙ Add a period.

Objective: Students edit, proofread, and publish their reports.

▶ **Writing a Persuasive Report for Adults**

Editing/Proofreading

Be sure to proofread your report. You don't want careless mistakes to distract your readers from your main ideas.

Conventions

☐ Did you check your spelling and punctuation?

☐ Did you use the correct forms of easily confused words such as *your* and *you're*?

☐ Do your sentence parts match? Do your subjects and verbs agree? Do your pronouns and antecedents agree? Do your modifiers match what they describe?

☐ Did you capitalize proper nouns and the first word in each sentence?

☐ Other _____

Publishing

Use this checklist to get your report ready for adult readers.

Presentation

☐ Make sure your writing is neat and your paragraphs are indented.

☐ Consider including a diagram, photograph, or other illustration to help readers understand the problem or your recommendation.

☐ Think of ways to share your report with your adult audience. For example, you might make copies and distribute them at a meeting of the PTA or the board of education. You could also send your report as a letter to the editor of a local newspaper.

☐ Other _____

Writing an Advertisement

Objective: Students prewrite their advertisements.

Use the writing process to write an advertisement directed at your parents or other adults.

Prewriting

Who is the audience for your ad?

☐ Your teacher

☐ A parent

☐ Adults in your neighborhood

☐ Other _____

What is your purpose for writing this ad?

☐ To persuade my audience to help stop polluting rivers and lakes

☐ To persuade my audience to help other adults learn to read

☐ Other _____

Name _____ Date _____

▶ **Writing an Advertisement**

Use this graphic organizer to organize your ad. Begin by writing what you want the adult or adults to do in the "Cause" circles. Then list the positive results of that action in the "Effect" circles.

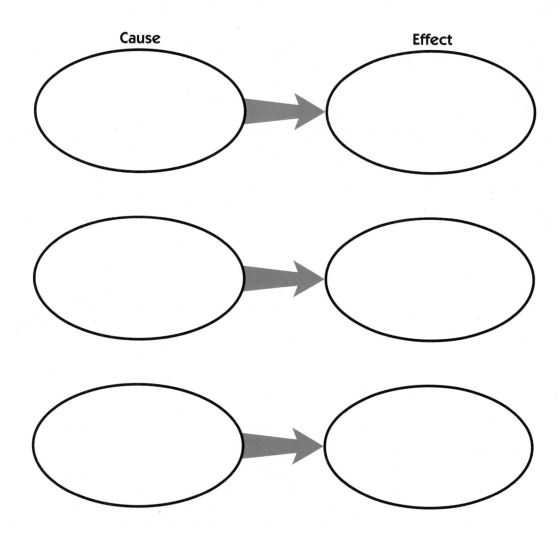

Cause   Effect

Drafting

Write a draft of your ad on loose-leaf paper or on a computer. Because it's an ad, you can express some of your ideas in words or phrases instead of sentences. Include a sketch of the illustration that might go in the ad. Keep a copy of your draft in your Writing Folder.

PERSUASIVE WRITING

UNIT 5   Communication • **Lesson 6** *My Two Drawings*

Objective: Students revise their advertisements.

> **Writing an Advertisement**

Revising

Read your ad carefully. Use this checklist to make it clearer and more convincing. Use proofreading marks to show any needed changes.

Ideas

☐ Did you clearly describe what you want your reader to do?

☐ Did you explain the most positive effects of supporting this cause or providing this service?

Organization

☐ Did you arrange your words, sentences, and illustrations so that they will grab your readers' attention?

Word Choice

☐ Did you express reasons to support this cause or provide this service with convincing words and pictures?

Sentence Fluency

☐ Did you read your ad aloud and listen for any awkward phrases or words?

Voice

☐ Will your adult reader know how important the cause or service in your ad is to you?

☐ Is your ad likely to convince readers to do as you suggested?

☐ Other _____

Rewrite your ad on loose-leaf paper or on a computer, making all the changes you marked on your draft.

Proofreading Marks

¶	Indent.
∧	Add something.
ℰ	Take something out.
∼	Transpose.
≡	Make a capital letter.
/	Make a small letter.
◯	Check spelling.
◠	Close up space.
#	Add space.
⊙	Add a period.

Objective: Students edit, proofread, and publish their advertisements.

PERSUASIVE WRITING

▶ **Writing an Advertisement**

Editing/Proofreading

Be sure to proofread your ad. You don't want careless mistakes to distract readers from your main ideas.

Conventions

☐ Make sure you spelled and capitalized any names or organizations correctly.

☐ Check for correct spelling.

☐ Make sure you used correct punctuation.

☐ Other _____

Publishing

Use this checklist to get your ad ready for adult readers.

Presentation

☐ Finish your ad by writing and drawing it by hand or on a computer.

☐ Make sure your ad is interesting and not too crowded. The art or illustration should go with the words and phrases in your ad.

☐ Think of ways to present your ad to your parent or another adult. For example, you could send it through the mail or make copies and post your ad in your neighborhood.

☐ Other _____

Writing a Quatrain

Use the writing process to write a quatrain.

Prewriting

Who is the audience for your poem?

☐ Other students at your school

☐ Your teacher

☐ Readers of a poetry magazine

☐ Other _____

What is your purpose for writing this poem?

☐ To express, in a poem, how the people in the colonies lived

☐ To capture, in a poem, the landscape of early America

☐ To express, in a poem, how Native Americans and the colonists worked together

☐ Other _____

Write some descriptive words and phrases that relate to the subject of your poem in the left column of the chart below. In the right column, list any rhyming pairs of words that you might use in your quatrain.

Descriptive Words	Rhyming Pairs

▶ **Writing a Quatrain**

Objective: Students prewrite and draft a quatrain.

P O E T R Y

Here's a quatrain from Myra Cohn Livingston's poem, "Lemonade Stand." Notice that lines 2 and 4 have end rhyme. Livingston chose not to rhyme lines 1 and 3.

> Plenty of sugar
> to make it sweet,
> and sometimes cookies
> for us to eat.

Look at the words you recorded on the previous page. Now form some of those words into a quatrain, following the pattern of "Lemonade Stand."

_____

_____

_____

_____

_____

_____

_____

_____

_____

_____

Drafting

Write the first draft of your poem on loose-leaf paper or on a computer. Refer to your prewriting notes to make sure you stay focused. Read the lines to yourself as you draft. Hearing the lines may help you discover rhythms and rhymes.

Name ______________________ Date __________

Writing a Quatrain

Objective: Students revise a quatrain.

Revising

Read the first draft of your poem. Then follow this checklist to improve your writing. Use proofreading marks as you make changes.

Ideas

- ☐ Do you stay focused on the subject of your poem?
- ☐ Do you create vivid images for your readers?

Organization

- ☐ Is your rhyme pattern consistent?
- ☐ Is your poem a quatrain?

Word Choice

- ☐ Do your words show rather than tell?
- ☐ Do your words fit the rhyme pattern of a quatrain?

Sentence Fluency

- ☐ Do you use a variety of phrases or sentences in your poem?

Voice

- ☐ Does the mood of your poem match the subject matter?

- ☐ Other ______________________________

Read through your revisions aloud to make sure your changes improved the poem. Then rewrite your poem on loose-leaf paper or on a computer.

Proofreading Marks

Mark	Meaning
¶	Indent.
^	Add something.
	Take something out.
~	Transpose.
≡	Make a capital letter.
/	Make a small letter.
sp	Check spelling.
⊂⊃	Close up space.
^#	Add space.
⊙	Add a period.

▶ **Writing a Quatrain**

Editing/Proofreading

Always proofread your revised drafts. Your final copy should be error-free. Use this checklist to make sure you remember to check everything.

Conventions

☐ Are all of your words spelled correctly?

☐ Is all punctuation correct and consistent within your poem?

☐ Do all proper nouns begin with a capital letter?

☐ Do you use capital letters or small letters consistently at the beginning of each line of poetry?

☐ Did you read your poem aloud to catch errors in rhythm or rhyme?

☐ Other _____

Publishing

Use this checklist to get your poem ready for publication.

Presentation

☐ Place your poem in your own Writing Folder.

☐ Neatly write or type a final copy on clean paper.

☐ Place the title of the poem at the top, in the center of the page. Center the poem on the page below the title.

☐ Send your poem to a magazine for publication or post it to a Web site that features poetry written by fourth-grade students.

☐ Organize a poetry reading with your classmates. Rehearse your poem until you are comfortable saying it aloud.

Objective: Students edit, proofread, and publish a quatrain.

POETRY

UNIT 6 A Changing America • **Lesson 2** *The Voyage of the Mayflower*

Writing a Cinquain

Objective: Students prewrite a cinquain.

Use the writing process to write a cinquain.

Prewriting

Who is the audience for your poem?

☐ Your classmates

☐ Your teacher

☐ Other _____

What is your purpose for writing this poem?

☐ To express ideas about the voyage of the *Mayflower* in a poem

☐ To describe the *Mayflower* in a poem

☐ To write a poem about the Pilgrims' struggle during their long journey on the *Mayflower*

☐ Other _____

In the space below, write down some things you know about the Pilgrims' journey to America on the *Mayflower*. Your ideas may be single words, phrases, or sentences.

_____

_____

_____

_____

_____

_____

UNIT 6 A Changing America • **Lesson 2** *The Voyage of the Mayflower*

▶ **Writing a Cinquain**

Use the pattern below to organize your cinquain. Try different words that might fit, and then choose the one that best expresses the subject of your poem. Circle the words you decide to use for each line of your cinquain.

Line 1	Write some words that name the subject of your cinquain here. _____ Then choose one word that names the subject. _____
Line 2	Write some words that describe the subject of your cinquain here. _____ Then choose two words that describe the subject. _____ _____
Line 3	Write some action words about the subject of your cinquain here. _____ Then choose three actions words about the subject. _____ _____ _____
Line 4	Write groups of two to four words that express a feeling or describe the subject. Each group should have six to eight syllables. _____ _____ Choose a group of words that express a feeling or describe the subject. _____
Line 5	Write some words that sum up the subject of your cinquain here. _____ Choose one word that sums up the subject. _____

Drafting

Write the first draft of your cinquain in cursive on loose-leaf paper or type it on a computer. Refer to prewriting plans as you write.

Objective: Students prewrite and draft a cinquain.

POETRY

Objective: Students revise a cinquain.

Writing a Cinquain

Revising

Read your cinquain. Use this checklist to make your poem better. Use proofreading marks as you make changes. Then ask a peer reviewer to read your poem as well. Talk about the changes you made.

Ideas

☐ Do you focus on one idea throughout the poem?

Organization

☐ Is the order of your words effective, or could you improve the poem by rearranging words?

☐ Do you follow the cinquain pattern?

Word Choice

☐ Do your words fit the pattern called for in a cinquain?

☐ Do you use precise words to describe the images in your poem?

☐ Do your words appeal to a variety of the readers' senses?

Voice

☐ Does the tone of your writing fit the subject of your poem?

☐ Other _____

Proofreading Marks	
¶	Indent.
∧	Add something.
ℯ	Take something out.
∼	Transpose.
≡	Make a capital letter.
/	Make a small letter.
ˢᵖ⌒	Check spelling.
⊂	Close up space.
#⌃	Add space.
⊙	Add a period.

Read your poem to yourself or to a partner. Listen for places in the poem that need improvement. When you have made all necessary changes, rewrite your poem on loose-leaf paper or on a computer.

Objective: Students edit, proofread, and publish a cinquain.

POETRY

> **Writing a Cinquain**

Editing/Proofreading

Always proofread a revised draft, no matter how carefully you rewrote it. Your final copy should be error-free. Use this checklist as you make final changes to your poem.

Conventions

☐ Are all words spelled correctly?

☐ Are all necessary commas in place?

☐ Do all proper nouns begin with a capital letter?

☐ Other _____

Publishing

Use this checklist to get your cinquain ready for publication for your teacher, a school newspaper, a class poetry collection, or a student literary magazine.

Presentation

☐ If you are handwriting, write a final copy on white paper. Center the poem on the page. Include your name following the poem.

☐ If you are working on computer, print a final copy on white paper. Use your word processor's tools to center the poem on the page. Experiment with fonts and font sizes until your poem looks the way you want it to.

☐ Read your work one more time. Correct any errors. Reprint if necessary.

☐ Create an illustration to be displayed with your cinquain.

Name _____ Date _____

Writing a Diamante

Use the writing process to write a diamante.

Prewriting

Who is the audience for your diamante?

☐ Other students in your school

☐ Your teacher

☐ Readers of a poetry magazine

☐ Other _____

What is your purpose?

☐ To record the deeds of a famous Native American

☐ To describe the qualities of a famous Native American

☐ To express your feelings about a famous Native American

☐ Other _____

Fill in the chart below with different types of nouns, adjectives, and participles you might use in your diamante. Use words that reflect the subject of your poem.

Nouns	Participles	Adjectives

▶ **Writing a Diamante**

Use the diamante pattern shown below to help you organize your poem. Fill in nouns, adjectives, and participles where indicated in the spaces below.

Line 1	Write 1 word—a noun
Line 2	Write 2 words—adjectives
Line 3	Write 3 words—participles
Line 4	Write 4 words—nouns
Line 5	Write 3 words—participles
Line 6	Write 2 words—adjectives
Line 7	Write 2 words—nouns

Objective: Students prewrite and draft a diamante.

P O E T R Y

Drafting

Write the first draft of your diamante in cursive on loose-leaf paper or type it on a computer. Rearrange words within each line so that the line flows smoothly or sounds good to your ear.

Objective: Students revise a diamante.

UNIT 6 A Changing America • **Lesson 3** *Pocahontas*

▶ **Writing a Diamante**

Revising

Read the draft of your diamante. Use this checklist to help you decide if there are areas you can improve. Use proofreading marks as you make changes.

Proofreading Marks

⁋	Indent.
∧	Add something.
ℓ	Take something out.
∼	Transpose.
≡	Make a capital letter.
/	Make a small letter.
ˢᵖ◯	Check spelling.
⊂⊃	Close up space.
∧#	Add space.
⊙	Add a period.

Ideas

☐ Is your poem focused, or do you create too many images?

☐ Does your poem express something, or is it just a list of words?

☐ Do you present images and ideas that your audience can understand?

Organization

☐ Does each line of your poem follow the diamante pattern?

Word Choice

☐ Do your words work together to create vivid images?

☐ Have you picked the best word for each line in your poem?

Voice

☐ What mood do your words create? Does it match the subject of your poem?

☐ Other _____

Read your poem aloud, with the revisions you've marked. When you are satisfied with your revisions, write a new copy of your diamante on loose-leaf paper or on a computer.

▶ **Writing a Diamante**

Objective: Students edit, proofread, and publish a diamante.

POETRY

Editing/Proofreading

Your final copy should be error-free, so it is important to proofread your revised draft, even for a short poem. Use this checklist to make sure you remember to check everything.

Conventions

☐ Did you double-check all words for correct spelling?

☐ Are all commas placed correctly?

☐ Do all proper nouns begin with a capital letter?

☐ Did you read your poem aloud to catch any awkward rhythms?

☐ Other _____

Publishing

Use this checklist to prepare your diamante for publication.

Presentation

☐ If you are working on a computer, print a final copy. Center the poem in the middle of the paper.

☐ If you are handwriting, write a final copy on white paper. Center the poem in the middle of the paper.

☐ Read your work one more time. Correct any errors.

☐ If you are sending your poem to a magazine, make sure you know the right format and address for the magazine.

☐ Organize a poetry reading with your classmates. Before you present your poem orally, rehearse until you know it by heart. Your delivery will be more effective if you don't have to read the poem.

Writing Free Verse

Objective: Students prewrite free-verse poetry.

Use the writing process to write free-verse poetry.

Prewriting

Who is the audience for your free-verse poem?

☐ Your teacher

☐ Other students in your school

☐ Other _____

What is your purpose?

☐ To relate, in a poem, something that happened during the Revolutionary War?

☐ To express, in a poem, your feelings about a historical figure or event?

☐ Other _____

In the space below, write some things you know or have read about the Revolutionary War.

_____

_____

_____

_____

_____

_____

_____

Name _____ Date _____

▶ **Writing Free Verse**

A web graphic organizer is a perfect tool for sorting out ideas prior to writing. Fill in the graphic below to organize your ideas for your free verse.

Objective: Students prewrite and draft free-verse poetry.

POETRY

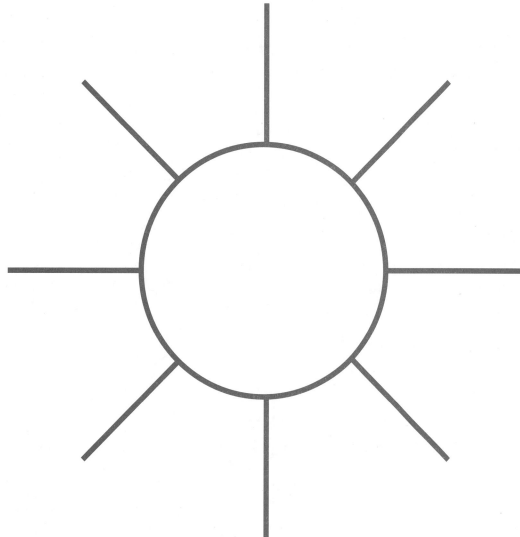

Drafting

Write the first draft of your poem in cursive. Use your prewriting notes to remind you of the images and feelings you want to express.

Objective: Students revise free-verse poetry.

▶ Writing Free Verse

Revising

Use this checklist to improve your writing. Use proofreading symbols to mark any changes.

Ideas

☐ Is the message of your poem clear?

☐ Do your words and images present one message, or do they present multiple messages?

Organization

☐ Are the details in your poem organized around one main idea?

☐ Do your line breaks make sense in the poem?

Word Choice

☐ Do you use interesting words to convey your feelings or message?

☐ Do your words appeal to readers' senses?

☐ Are your words arranged so that your poem is interesting to read?

Voice

☐ Does the style of your writing match your topic?

☐ Will the voice of your poem interest your audience?

☐ Other _____

Proofreading Marks	
¶	Indent.
∧	Add something.
ℓ	Take something out.
⁓	Transpose.
≡	Make a capital letter.
/	Make a small letter.
⟋ sp	Check spelling.
⊂⊃	Close up space.
#	Add space.
⊙	Add a period.

Read your revised poem aloud to test its sound and its flow. Then rewrite your poem on loose-leaf paper or on a computer, making all revisions.

Objective: Students edit, proofread, and publish free-verse poetry.

POETRY

▶ Writing Free Verse

Editing/Proofreading

Proofreading carefully is the final step in creating an error-free final copy. Use this checklist to make sure you remember to check everything.

Conventions

☐ Are all words spelled correctly?

☐ Is all punctuation correct?

☐ Did you use a consistent system for capitalizing words?

☐ If you use a specialized format (such as indenting or spacing lines or words out for effect) for your poem, is it consistent throughout?

☐ Other _____

Publishing

Use this checklist to get your poem ready for publication.

Presentation

☐ Display poems on a bulletin board that includes historical information about the Revolutionary War.

☐ Hold a poetry reading for students studying American history. Rehearse your poem in front of at least one other person until you are completely comfortable presenting it.

☐ Print out or write a neat, clean final copy on white paper.

☐ Read your work one more time to make sure there are no errors in the final copy.

Name _____ Date _____

Objective: Students prewrite pattern poetry.

Writing a Pattern Poem

Use the writing process to write a pattern poem.

Prewriting

Who is the audience for your pattern poem?

☐ Your teacher

☐ Other students interested in the subject of your pattern poem

☐ Readers of a poetry magazine

☐ Other _____

What is your purpose?

☐ To tell, in a poem, about something that might have happened to a nineteenth-century settler

☐ To tell, in a poem, what life was like on a wagon train

☐ Other _____

Here is the first verse of "The Ants Go Marching One by One." You may use this poem as the basis for your pattern poem.

The ants go marching one by one—hurrah! hurrah!
The ants go marching one by one—hurrah! hurrah!
The ants go marching one by one,
    the little one stops to suck his thumb,
    and they all go marching down, below, the earth.

POETRY

Objective: Students prewrite and draft pattern poetry.

▶ Writing a Pattern Poem

Fill in the chart below to organize your ideas for your pattern poem. Follow the pattern of "The Ants Go Marching One by One" or choose another poem you have read.

The ants go marching one by one—hurrah! hurrah!	Write line 1 here. _____ _____
The ants go marching one by one—hurrah! hurrah!	Write line 2 here. _____ _____
The ants go marching one by one,	Write line 3 here. _____ _____
the little one stops to suck his thumb,	Write line 4 here. _____ _____
and they all go marching down, below, the earth.	Write line 5 here. _____ _____

Drafting

Write the first draft of your pattern poem on loose-leaf paper or on a computer. Refer to your prewriting chart as you write your draft.

Name _____ Date _____

Objective: Students revise pattern poetry.

Revising

**Use the questions in this checklist to help
you think about—and improve—your draft.
Use proofreading marks to make changes.**

Ideas

☐ Does your poem provide insight or give
interesting information about nineteenth-
century settlers?

☐ Does your poem have a clear message?

Organization

☐ If you composed more than one verse, are
your verses consistent in format?

Word Choice

☐ Do the words you chose fit the poem's rhythm
easily?

☐ Are the words you chose meaningful and
descriptive?

Voice

☐ Do your words, rhythm, and message combine to create
an interesting composition?

☐ Other _____

**Read your revised work aloud to make sure you caught
everything that needs to be changed. Then create a new
copy of your pattern poem on loose-leaf paper or on a
computer.**

	Proofreading Marks
¶	Indent.
∧	Add something.
ℯ	Take something out.
∼	Transpose.
≡	Make a capital letter.
/	Make a small letter.
⟳	Check spelling.
⊂⊃	Close up space.
#	Add space.
⊙	Add a period.

Objective: Students edit, proofread, and publish pattern poetry.

POETRY

▶ **Writing a Pattern Poem**

Editing/Proofreading

It is important to proofread your revised draft. Your final copy should be error-free. Use this checklist to make sure you remember to check everything. Work with a peer reviewer so that you can proofread each other's writing.

Conventions

☐ Are all words spelled correctly?

☐ Is all punctuation correct?

☐ Does each sentence begin with a capital letter?

☐ Do all proper nouns begin with a capital letter?

☐ Are there any inconsistencies in punctuation or format?

☐ Other _____

Publishing

Use this checklist to get your pattern poem ready for publication. Following are some publishing options:

Presentation

☐ Print out or write a final copy on clean white paper.

☐ Read your poem one more time to make sure you didn't create any new errors in the final copy.

☐ If submitting your poem to the school newspaper, find out exactly what format the editor prefers.

☐ If preparing for an oral reading, rehearse your poem until you can recite it comfortably and naturally.

☐ Create or photocopy illustrations or photographs to display with the poem, if appropriate.

☐ Display the poem on a bulletin board about westward expansion.

Writing an Observation Report

Objective: Students prewrite an observation report.

Use the writing process to write an observation report.

Prewriting

Who is the audience for your observation report?

☐ Your class

☐ Other students in your school

☐ Yourself

☐ Other _____

What is your purpose?

☐ To relate the results of an experiment

☐ To inform readers about the properties of a metal or mineral

☐ To record information about a science experiment to use in an oral presentation

☐ Other _____

Briefly describe the experiment you will conduct. Include a list of materials and the procedure you will follow. Include your thoughts about what you might observe or learn.

_____

_____

_____

_____

_____

Objective: Students prewrite and draft an observation report.

DESCRIPTIVE WRITING

▶ Writing an Observation Report

A chain-of-events graphic organizer is one tool you can use to record the steps in an experiment. Fill in the organizer below to order your notes on an experiment you have read about or observed.

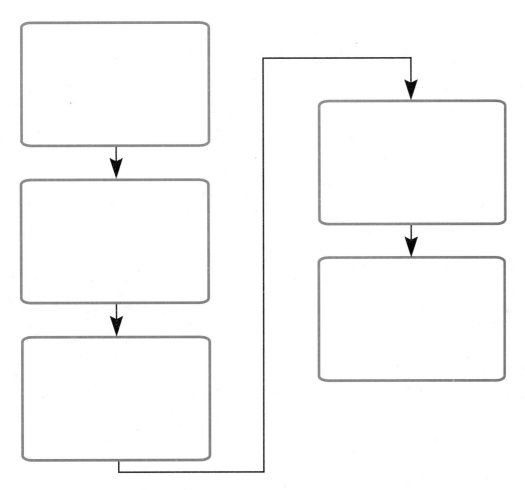

Drafting

Write the first draft of your observation report on loose-leaf paper or on a computer. Refer to your notes as well as to the graphic organizer you completed to make sure you report all details.

UNIT 6 **A Changing America • Lesson 6** *The California Gold Rush*

Writing an Observation Report

Revising

Read the draft of your observation report. If possible, do so with a classmate. Use this checklist to improve your work. Use proofreading marks as you make changes.

Ideas

☐ Do you tell your readers both what you did and what you observed?

Organization

☐ Do you use a logical method of organization, such as time order, left to right, or top to bottom?

☐ Does your report clearly identify the procedure, your observations, and your conclusions?

Word Choice

☐ Are your words precise so your readers can relate to the observations?

Sentence Fluency

☐ Do you use a variety of sentence styles to keep your writing interesting?

☐ Do you use signal words to connect ideas, sentences, and paragraphs?

Voice

☐ Does your report sound as if you actually made the observations?

☐ Other _____

Rewrite your observation report on loose-leaf paper or on a computer making all revisions.

Proofreading Marks	
¶	Indent.
∧	Add something.
ℓ	Take something out.
∼	Transpose.
≡	Make a capital letter.
/	Make a small letter.
⌢ sp	Check spelling.
⌒	Close up space.
∧#	Add space.
⊙	Add a period.

Objective: Students revise an observation report.

Writing an Observation Report

DESCRIPTIVE WRITING

Editing/Proofreading

Editing and proofreading are especially important in a scientific report. Use this checklist to make sure you check everything in your report.

Conventions

☐ Make sure that all words are correctly spelled.

☐ Check all punctuation to make sure it is correct.

☐ Make sure that each sentence and all proper nouns begin with a capital letter.

☐ Look for and correct any grammatical errors such as sentence fragments, run-on sentences, and misplaced modifiers.

☐ Other _____

Publishing

Use this checklist to get your observation report ready for publication. Some publishing options are as follows:

Presentation

☐ Create an appropriate chart, table, or graph that presents or summarizes information in your report. Use computer software, if available.

☐ If working on a computer, print a final copy of your report on white paper.

☐ If handwriting, write a final copy on white paper.

☐ Present the report at a science fair or science competition.

☐ Set up a science display case that includes the experiment apparatus and your report.

Objective: Students prewrite a description.

Writing a Description

Use the writing process to write a description.

Prewriting

Who is the audience for your description?

☐ Your classmates

☐ Other students in your school

☐ Your teacher

☐ Parents or other grown-ups

☐ Other _____

What is your purpose for writing?

☐ To describe one of the first trains that traveled across the United States

☐ To describe an old steam-powered train

☐ To describe a modern-day train

☐ Other _____

What are you going to describe?

_____

_____

What method of organization have you chosen? Why did you choose that method to describe your train?

_____

_____

Name _____ Date _____

▶ **Writing a Description**

Use the web graphic organizer to organize the details of
your description. You can then use those categories
when you write your draft.

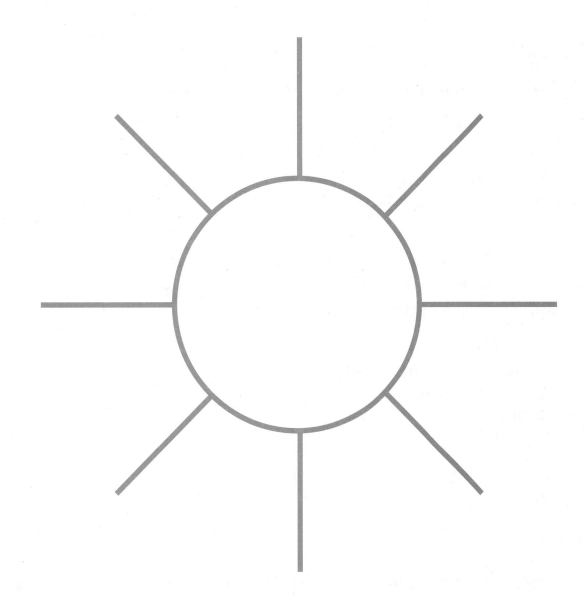

Drafting

Write the first draft of your description on loose-leaf
paper or on a computer. Use the ideas you recorded in
your graphic organizer and stick to your chosen method
of organization.

Objective: Students prewrite and draft a description.

DESCRIPTIVE WRITING

Objective: Students revise a description.

Writing a Description

Revising

Use this checklist to improve your work. Use proofreading marks as you make changes.

Ideas

☐ Are the details in your description original and informative?

☐ Is your description interesting and engaging?

Organization

☐ Do you follow a single method of organization?

☐ Do you use signal words to let readers know how you are describing the object?

Word Choice

☐ Do you use precise, vivid words that really show what the object looks like?

☐ Do your words appeal to your readers' senses?

Sentence Fluency

☐ Do you use signal words to help your ideas flow from sentence to sentence and from paragraph to paragraph?

Voice

☐ Does your writing sound as if you are actually interested in this object?

☐ Other _____

Then create a new copy of your description on loose-leaf paper or on a computer making all revisions.

Proofreading Marks	
¶	Indent.
∧	Add something.
℮	Take something out.
∼	Transpose.
≡	Make a capital letter.
/	Make a small letter.
⌢	Check spelling.
⌒	Close up space.
#	Add space.
⊙	Add a period.

Objective: Students edit, proofread, and publish a description.

▶ Writing a Description

DESCRIPTIVE WRITING

Editing/Proofreading

Always proofread your work. Your final product should not have any errors in it. Use this checklist to make sure you check everything.

Conventions

☐ Are all words spelled correctly?

☐ Does each sentence begin with a capital letter?

☐ Do all proper nouns begin with a capital letter?

☐ Is all punctuation correct?

☐ Did you look for and correct any grammatical errors such as sentence fragments, run-on sentences, and misplaced modifiers?

☐ Other _____

Publishing

Use this checklist to get your observation report ready for publication. You may use this description as part of a longer report for a social studies or history report. Or, this description may be part of a fictional story.

Presentation

☐ If working on a computer, print a final copy on white paper.

☐ If handwriting, write a final copy on white paper.

☐ Read your work one more time. Neatly correct any errors you made in the final copy.

☐ You may wish to include a photograph or photocopy of a picture of the object with your description.

Cumulative Checklists

Ideas

- [ ] Is each step clearly written?
- [ ] Do you leave out any important steps or information?
- [ ] Do you write about the main idea in the book, story, or article you read?
- [ ] Do you include only the most important details in your summary?

Organization

- [ ] Have you written a short introduction to tell readers what you are explaining?
- [ ] Do you use organizational strategy, such as sequential order, chronological order, order of importance, top-to-bottom, or left-to-right organization?
- [ ] Have you added a short conclusion to your explanation?
- [ ] Does the topic sentence of your summary explain the main idea of the selection?
- [ ] Do the other sentences in the paragraph support the main idea?
- [ ] Do you organize the background information in the body in a logical way?
- [ ] Have you ended with a sentence that summarizes your story or includes your observations?

Revising

Word Choice

☐ Do you include words that show the order of the steps in the process?

☐ Do you name any parts or tools correctly?

☐ Have you chosen the best words to explain the main idea and details in the book, story, or article?

☐ Do you use words, such as *first*, *next*, and *last*, that show the order of events in your autobiography?

Sentence Fluency

☐ Does each sentence lead to the next one, with no sudden jumps from one topic to a new one?

☐ Do you combine short sentences when possible?

Voice

☐ Did you explain why this process is important to readers?

☐ Does your explanation show that you are interested in this process?

☐ Can the reader tell that you have read the book, story, or article you summarized?

Editing/Proofreading

Unit 1 Grammar and Usage

Lesson 1	☐	Nouns
Lesson 2	☐	Plural and Possessive Nouns
Lesson 3	☐	Pronouns
Lesson 4	☐	Verbs
Lesson 5	☐	What Is a Sentence?
Lesson 6	☐	Kinds of Sentences
Lesson 7	☐	Review

Unit 2 Grammar, Usage, and Mechanics

Lesson 1	☐	Types of Sentences
Lesson 2	☐	Capitalization
Lesson 3	☐	Periods and End Punctuation
Lesson 4	☐	Commas
Lesson 5	☐	Quotation Marks and Underlining
Lesson 6	☐	Colons, Semicolons, and Hyphens
Lesson 7	☐	Review

Unit 3 Grammar, Usage, and Mechanics

Lesson 1	☐	Apostrophes
Lesson 2	☐	Verb Tenses
Lesson 3	☐	Subject-Verb Agreement
Lesson 4	☐	Pronoun-Antecedent Agreement
Lesson 5	☐	Intensive, Reflexive, and Demonstrative Pronouns
Lesson 6	☐	Adjectives and Adverbs
Lesson 7	☐	Review

Editing/Proofreading

Unit 4 Grammar and Usage

Lesson 1 ☐ Comparative and Superlative Adjectives
Lesson 2 ☐ Comparative and Superlative Adverbs
Lesson 3 ☐ Conjunctions and Interjections
Lesson 4 ☐ Prepositions
Lesson 5 ☐ Double Negatives and Contractions
Lesson 6 ☐ Review

Unit 5 Grammar and Usage

Lesson 1 ☐ Phrases
Lesson 2 ☐ Clauses
Lesson 3 ☐ Direct Objects
Lesson 4 ☐ Fragments, Run-On, Rambling, and Awkward Sentences
Lesson 5 ☐ Agreement in Sentences
Lesson 6 ☐ Review

Unit 6 Grammar, Usage, and Mechanics

Lesson 1 ☐ Parts of Speech
Lesson 2 ☐ Capitalization and Punctuation
Lesson 3 ☐ Words, Phrases and Clauses
Lesson 4 ☐ Understanding and Combining Sentences
Lesson 5 ☐ Common Irregular Verbs
Lesson 6 ☐ Past, Present and Future Tenses
Lesson 7 ☐ Review

Cumulative Checklists

Unit 2 Expository Writing

☐ Share your explanation of process with others. Publish a newsletter and, then, distribute the newsletter to other kids in your school.

☐ If you write about a process, such as how to start a dog walking business, do it! You might need help from your parents or your teacher before you start your business.

☐ Share your summary with others. You and your classmates might combine summaries of similar selections into folders. Label each folder to tell readers what kind of summaries it contains. Put the folders in your school library or classroom for others to read and use for a book or research report.

☐ Give an oral presentation of your research report to your class. Use illustrations, charts, diagrams, or tables in your presentation.

Unit 3 Personal Writing

☐ Make sure your typing or writing is neat, with no crossed-out words.

☐ Sign your letter.

☐ Address and proofread the envelope. Make sure the address is correct and matches the heading on your letter.

Unit 4 Narrative Writing

☐ Include illustrations or photographs. Present them neatly by pasting onto a sheet of paper or by scanning and placing them in your electronic file.

☐ Send your narrative to a newspaper or magazine for possible publication. Make sure you have followed the publication's rules for preparing your writing for publication.

☐ Make a collection of tall tales. Bind your tall tale in a book with those of your classmates.

Publishing

☐ If you are going to submit the biography to a magazine or web site, find out exactly what format the editor or publisher requires.

☐ Perform a play you've written before an audience.

Unit 5 Persuasive Writing

☐ Think of several ways to share your paragraph with people outside the classroom. For example, you could send it to the school or community newspaper or e-mail it to someone who is interested in your topic.

☐ Make sure your ad is interesting to look at and not too crowded. Consider using color and perhaps computer clip-art.

☐ Brainstorm several ways to make sure potential customers see your ad. For example, you might make it into a poster or a flyer. Perhaps your neighborhood has a newsletter that would print your ad.

Unit 6 Poetry and Descriptive Writing

☐ Send your poem to a magazine for publication or post it to a web site that features poetry written by fourth-grade students.

☐ Organize a poetry reading with your classmates. Rehearse your poem until you are comfortable saying it aloud.

☐ If your poem is for your portfolio, write a paragraph about the process of the writing the poem. What did you learn? What might you do differently next time?

☐ Create an appropriate chart, table, or graph that presents or summarizes information in your report. Use computer software, if available.